If I Had Wings,
These Windmills Would Be Dead.

Written by Chuck Howe

Cover and Book Design
by Erin McParland

Edited
by Emilie Rappoport
and Bud Smith

Some stories in this book have appeared online at Redfez.org and Theweekendersmagazine.com. "The Yellow Barn" and "Einfahrt Freihalten" have appeared in "Uno Kudo" Volumes 1 and 2 respectively. "Two Weeks" appears in "First Time".

UNKNOWN PRESS
Copyright © 2013 All rights reserved.
This book, or parts thereof, may not be reproduced in any form without permission.

DEDICATIONS

*Dedicated to the memory of Sil, Melissa, Jason, Dave R,
Dave P, Scott, Aaron, Maggie, CJ, Grandpa Tenace, Harold and Dottie,
Pig Pen, Thurman Munson and Gene's Iguana*

"When I had no wings to fly, you flew to me"

–Robert Hunter "Attics of my Life"

Table of Contents:

1. The Swing
2. Blame Mom
3. Caldor
4. Gizzert Bones
5. The British are Coming
6. Sharp Dressed Man
7. Pinch Hitter
8. Mags
9. Miss Delvecchio
10. Charlie Hustle
11. Puppy Love
12. Cobra v. Mongoose
13. The Piss Test
14. Pyrotechnics
15. Battlefield Bedford
16. Machete
17. Buses and Blunts
18. The Swing's Revenge
19. Frisbee
20. Authority Song
21. Two Weeks
22. Yellow Barn
23. Crash of '91
24. Ballroom Gin
25. Call The Dogs
26. Nantucket
27. Burning of Nag Champa
28. Laughter
29. End of Summer

30. The Guru
31. Phish Tour
32. Canadian Mule
33. Harmful or Fatal if Swallowed
34. The Ballad of Rich and Rebecca
35. The House on the Ridge
36. The Naked Chick
37. The Ballad of Rich and Rebecca Part II
38. Kentucky Fried Pete
39. Party Time
40. Sunrise
41. Sing Sing
42. Merde d'Jour
43. Curried Eggs and National Steel
44. Cindy
45. Because We Have a Fucking Gig Tonight
46. The Sailor
47. Reunion
48. Married
49. Barstools and Dreamers
50. Walkers
51. Sao Paulo Shuffle
52. Einfahrt Friehalten
53. Enjoying the Ride
54. Al
55. The Vibes
56. Solo

The Swing

I still remember the day as if it were yesterday instead of the summer of 1977. I was playing on the tire swing in the front yard. My brother was off playing with his friends. My father was cutting 2 by 4s in the backyard. It was the last time those poor pieces of wood would see the light of day, soon to be covered up with sheet rock. My mother was in the house, doing whatever mothers do in the summer when the kids are outside playing.

I was pumping my legs hard, going higher and higher in the swing. Still the pale blue sky was out of my reach. I had been trying all summer, but I hadn't been able to touch the sky. This time I would do it. Each time up, the swing went higher. Finally, I jumped as the swing was at its highest point. Surely I could touch the sky this time.

I jumped. I flew straight up. The common pull of gravity was gone, completely gone. I had to twist myself around to dodge the power lines and branches of the tree, but I quickly shot past them. I could see the sky getting closer and closer, but I was slowing down. I looked down and could see my house and neighborhood far below me. I was almost there. This time I would do it. This time I would touch the sky.

Just as I felt myself losing all momentum, about to fall back to the ground, the very tip of my fingers touched it. It was like the softest velvet I had ever felt. The sky felt warm, and almost plush, like a stuffed animal. The sky was right there, on my fingertips, for just a brief moment, but the moment seemed to last for an hour. And then I started falling back to earth. Slowly at first, but I picked up speed as I fell. The ground was coming fast. My town turned into my neighborhood, my neighborhood turned into my street, my street turned into my yard and then slam, my feet hit the ground. I felt the shock wave in my ankles and stood there stunned for a second. I had finally done it; I had finally touched the sky. I went running to the back yard to tell my father. Surely this news would brighten his day.

Blame Mom

I was three or four and I thought I had gotten the whole "walking" thing down. I had been doing it for half my life, no problems. I felt fully capable of walking to my neighbor's house to see if he wanted to come out and play. I noticed my neighbor's flagstone front step was approaching my face awfully fast.

Bang!

"Waaaaaaa!"

Next thing I knew I was sitting with my mom in the emergency room with a completely flattened nose. The Doctor came in, took a look at me and flinched. It must have been bad.

"What happened here?" the Doctor asked all doctorly.

"Well he was," my mom started to answer but the Doctor quickly cut her off.

"I want HIM to tell me," the Doctor quickly snapped at her, in almost an angry tone. My mom looked a little startled. I told the Doctor that I slipped at my neighbor's. He then asked my mom for an old picture so he could try to make my nose look like it used to. I would need surgery.

When the Doctor left I asked my mom why I had to answer him when he asked what had happened. "Well, he wanted to make sure I didn't do it to you. Isn't that funny?"

Yes. Funny, very funny. Why would my mom break my nose? The more I thought about it, the funnier it seemed. Why would Mom, the woman who tells me not to stick the fork in the electric outlet, break my nose? Hysterical.

A couple of days later I was with my mom at the supermarket. I must have looked like a little alien child. I had a big plastic mask over my nose that was taped to my face and two badly blackened eyes. I didn't give a shit; I was still running all over trying to put the Boo-Berry in my mom's cart before she noticed.

At one point I went running around the corner of the aisle and ran face first into a man's leg. "Ow!" I yelled holding my nose, not really hurt, but reminded of my injury.

"Oh, you had better watch where you are going young man." He was a kind old man with a great big smile, and when he noticed my face mask and black eyes, he was a little startled but still smiling. "Oh my, what happened to you?"

He looked like a friendly, happy guy. I was sure he'd probably appreciate a good joke, and I had just heard the best one ever. Right as my mom came around the corner, I answered loudly and with a big smile, "My mom did it."

Caldor

Every Saturday my Dad would pull my brother and me away from our cartoons to go somewhere. It was somewhere different all the time. Most of the time they were just trips because he needed to get something and to give my Mom some quiet time at home while we were out. Once a month it would be the dump with a carload of building scrap. Sometimes it would be the hardware store, or if we got really lucky, Caldor.

Once when I was four, my brother was already outside playing, so my father just grabbed me. The point was usually to just get us out of my Mom's hair for awhile, and since my brother was playing outside he was already out of her hair. I got lucky this time too, it was a Caldor trip. He needed a new tool or something, but it meant I got to check out all the Matchbox cars and Star Wars figures, or the latest 45s or even the candy section.

He found a spot right out in front and I went running straight to the toy section, my father shouting that he would be in the tool section if I needed him. I barely paid attention. Toys. Why would I need him? First I noticed the matchbox cars. They were cool, but since my brother or I had most of the coolest ones already, I moved on to Star Wars.

Again I was disappointed. I already had most of their selection. Nothing too exciting was going on with Nerf either and that took me into sporting goods. My brother would have been in sporting goods if he had come, but other than the BB Guns that I wasn't allowed to have yet anyway, there was no reason for me to go to sporting goods. But I swung a few baseball bats and bounced a few basketballs anyway.

I went through the record section. I was still a few months away from hearing Thick as Brick for the first time, so at that point I was only interested in Donnie and Marie, Elvis and the Beatles. There was definitely nothing new from the Beatles. Elvis may have still been alive, for the next few weeks or so anyway, but nothing caught my eye. I checked out the books, the magazines, the candy aisle, everything. Slowly it dawned on me that my father hadn't come to pull me away from the absolutely nothing good that I was finding.

Chuck Howe

So I actually made my way to the tools. I had to pass a lot of sections to get there. Household appliances. Automotive. Lawn and Garden. I took my time and played with everything I saw. When I got to tools, my father was nowhere to be found. Maybe he had gone to look for me in toys while I was pretending the lawn chairs were thrones, so I walked back to toys. He wasn't there. I was confused. He had to be somewhere. I hadn't checked in clothes, there was no reason for him to be there, but maybe he was. Besides, it was fun to climb into the circular racks and scare old women looking at clearance dresses. Still no sign of Dad though.

I was beginning to get worried. What if Dad had talked to a stranger and been kidnapped? I did what my Mom would have done if she couldn't find me in toys; I went up to the front desk.

"Excuse me; I think my Dad got lost." I told the nice looking woman behind the desk.

"And what's your Dad's name?" she asked.

"Dad," I replied with complete certainty I had answered correctly.

She paused. "And what's YOUR name."

"Chuck."

She spoke into a microphone that sent her voice all over the huge store. "Will Chuck's Dad please come to the courtesy desk? Chuck's Dad to the courtesy desk please." We waited. No Dad. "Will Chuck's Dad please come to the courtesy desk?" she repeated, beginning to look a little worried herself. More time passed. She was just about to make the announcement again when Dad came walking over.

"Oh, there you are. I've been looking all over for you." I apologized, because obviously I wasn't where I was supposed to be. We got in the car and headed home.

As we pulled in the driveway, my Mom came running from the kitchen. She grabbed me and kissed me and hugged me and wanted to know if I was OK. I thought she was acting really weird, but I said I was fine and ran off to play with my brother.

It was later that I found out the my father had left Caldor with his brand new tools, eager to get to work on the house. As he pulled down the street, he saw my brother, but not me. He pulled up to my brother and asked, "Did I take Chuck to Caldor with me?"

If I Had Wings These Windmills Would Be Dead

"Yes." He replied.

"Don't tell your Mom," he yelled out the window as he turned the car around.

As soon as he was headed up the road, my brother ran to the house yelling "Mom-Mom-Dad left Chuck at Caldor!"

Gizzert Bones

I looked at the plate. I had eaten most of the meat, but the carrots and potatoes sat there, untouched. My father was in the den, watching the Yankees. My brother was in his room, reading his Sports Illustrated. My mom was with me in the kitchen, waiting and waiting.

"Do I have to?"

"Finish it. All of it," she replied like she meant it. She had already finished all of the dishes, except for mine. I felt like I had been sitting there for two hours, and I probably had been. I pushed the potatoes around the plate, but I couldn't bring myself to actually put them in my mouth. They were cold. Cold potatoes, I thought, would make me physically ill. Their texture caused me to gag uncontrollably. I couldn't understand why my mom would torture me in such a way.

My brother came into the kitchen and poured himself a tall glass of milk. He opened the cookie drawer and took out the Chips Ahoy. He smiled at me, knowing full well I wanted Chips Ahoy a whole lot more than I wanted the poisonous, cold potatoes. He sat at the table and dunked a cookie in the milk. After he took a bite he smiled and licked his lips.

"Mmm, cookies are so good," he dunked another and made an even bigger deal about how good they were.

"Mom!" I yelled.

"Jacky, don't tease your brother," she said halfheartedly and then turned to me, "And you! Finish your dinner and you can have dessert."

I quickly choked down one of the remaining potatoes, gagging and coughing and making a huge act of it. That was it. I could stand no more. I took my napkin off my lap and threw it on my plate.

"I'm done."

"No, you are not. You still have a carrot and two potatoes."

"Nope, I am done. No more dinner. My dinner bones have gone away, my gizzert bones are in."

My mom looked at me in disbelief. "Your gizzert bones?"

"Yup, I can't eat dinner if my gizzert bones are in. But I could eat a cookie."

She almost broke down laughing. She did the only thing she could. She handed me a Chips Ahoy. "One, then right to bed."

Every night from then on I would try the gizzert bones trick, but it never worked again.

The British are Coming

My parents never found out about it, but my house helped save the universe many times when I was growing up. You see, we lived in a special house. Our house could transform.

There were several different ways I could transform the house. From the third floor TV room, the house could transform into a rocket ship and blast off into space. In later years, thanks to the advanced operating systems of its Atari 5200 brain core and the program called Xaxxon, weapons systems became so advanced I could wipe out entire alien worlds.

From the front porch I could activate the fort mode whenever Indians or the British would attack. A gun could easily be put between the slats to fire on the enemy, and there was no way they could fire on you. How could they see you inside the fort? They were sitting ducks. A lesser used function of the porch was the transporter module. If four people were sitting around the white painted, wrought iron, glass top table and all held on to the iron loops and concentrated really hard, the house would be transported to any place and time we desired. Once we made the mistake of going to the moon without space suits. We almost suffocated before we made it back.

From the basement I could activate submarine mode, and earth core drill mode. Both were good for rainy days. Of course I had to kill all of the green aliens who lived in the furnace before it was safe enough to operate any of the basement controls, so that put a bit of a damper on it all.

My favorite transformation could only be activated late at night and from my bedroom, from in my bed to be more specific. Once I pressed the right combination of buttons (in the design of the wallpaper) on the wall, the house would transform into a giant robotic monster. Of course, my room was the beast's head. The monster could shoot rockets, breathe fire and his armor was a million inches thick. The poor sleepy town of Mount Kisco endured many nights of horror as this great monster made its way through town, destroying everything in its path. All of the citizens would then have to run out and work all night to make the town presentable again by morning.

Chuck Howe

Of course, on the occasion where aliens would invade, or another monster attacked the town, all the town's people would turn to the great robot monster to save them. And when I was at the controls, we never failed.

Sharp Dressed Man

It was going to be a great night. My aunt was picking me up and taking me out to dinner. Me. Just me. Not me and my brother. Not the whole family. Me. My mother had not yet learned that she had to choose her words very carefully with me. "Go upstairs and put on your best clothes."

My best clothes. A normal human would think, "Nice shirt, nice pants." Not me. I took best to mean my favorite. The Superman Underoos were an obvious choice, but next I needed pants. I skipped right over the plaid slacks that my mother meant. Instead I found the yellow football pants that came with the Los Angeles Rams jersey and helmet that I got for Christmas. I wasn't really a Rams fan, but their helmet was really trippy. I liked trippy things even as a little kid. They were bright yellow, no one wore bright yellow pants, so to me, they were my best pants.

The t-shirt was a harder choice. On the one hand I had the white shirt with a picture of a chimpanzee on it. The words "Mucho Macho" were written around his head. I had seen Mucho Macho live and in person at a roadside attraction in Florida. Mucho Macho was even cooler than King Kong.

On the other hand I had the black t-shirt I had bought with my own money at the Denim Mine in the mall after seeing the movie Grease. In case I ever ran into Olivia Newton John, I wanted her to know that I was her type of guy, so I had them put the word "Greaser" on back in white, velour, iron-on letters. Was there a chance Olivia Newton John would be at the Mount Kisco Diner that night? Probably not, but if she were there, I would be so disappointed if I didn't wear the Greaser shirt. The black greaser shirt won.

The hat was another easy decision. Second choice would have been my Cincinnati Reds hat. It had a big white C for Chuck on it. But that wasn't good enough; it had to be my coon-skin cap. My neighbor's boyfriend, a big high school kid, had a coon tail on the antennae of his car. He must have been cool as hell. I was going to have a car like that one day too, but until then, I had my cap. Since the first moment

Chuck Howe

I saw Fess Parker in Disney's Davy Crockett, I needed a coon-skin cap. I don't know where my mom found it, but that was a dream that had come true.

Yellow pants, black greaser shirt and coon skin cap. I looked good, but I still didn't look my best. I was missing something. It dawned on me suddenly. I took off running for the basement. As I ran passed my mom and dad they burst out in laughter. I was just a black and yellow blur with a tail on my head. In the basement I ran straight to my father's workbench. I looked around and found them. A giant pair of safety goggles. I put them on. Perfect. I didn't need to look in a mirror; I knew these were my best clothes by far.

I went upstairs. My mom, through her stifled laughter tried to tell me to go up and change, but when she saw how proud of my outfit I was, she couldn't help saying how great I looked. My Aunt pulled up and I ran out to the car to meet her. She almost threw up, she was trying to hold back her laughter so hard. She looked up at my parents but they were no help. All she could do was open the car door and take me to the diner.

Pinch Hitter

I heard my brother say he was getting ready to go outside to throw the ball. That meant throw the ball against the fence to practice his pitching motion. But that also meant he would be working and wouldn't want to be bothered by me. That sucked. I had to do something about it.

I ran outside and to the garage. Something in there would save me. Something would make him pay attention to me instead of throwing the ball at the fence over and over. My eyes locked on the shovel hanging on the wall. I grabbed it and ran to the back yard. My brother still hadn't come out yet. It would be too obvious if I started digging right where he threw, but if I moved three feet to the left and dug along the fence ... Perfect. If I started now I could even yell for mom that he was bothering me.

I started digging furiously. I wanted it to look like I had been at it for a while. I got two minutes worth of digging in before he came out with his glove and bucket of balls. "What are you doing?"
"Digging." "Digging for what?"
"Dinosaur bones."
"Dinosaur bones?"
"Yup."
"Right here? Dinosaur bones?"
"Yup. Got a feeling about this spot."
"I was gonna practice pitching."
"Gotta dig. Gotta find the dinosaur bones."
"Mom ..." He turned around and went back inside. Mom never came out to tell me to stop. I kept digging for about an hour. Finally I got sick of it. The hole was only about a foot and a half deep, even though I felt like I had dug to China. I went inside. My brother didn't say a thing to me; he just went outside with his glove and balls.

The next morning when I went outside I was surprised to see a new bush planted in my hole. I could just see my brother the day before telling my mom that I was digging a hole.

"Where?"

"By the fence."

"I have a new plant that would look good there. Let him keep digging."

MAGS

It was the greatest day ever in the history of all adolescent boys who have ever lived on Captain Merritt's hill. At some point in the early morning, someone put Mr. Richard's entire porno collection in a box and put it out on the curb.

It was early in the morning on one of the last days of summer before school. My neighbor, Rawley, and I were out riding bikes, enjoying our soon to be doomed freedom. There was a new box on the otherwise pristine suburban street and we went straight for it. I could swear the top of the box began to glow as we opened it and peered inside. Playboy, Hustler, Penthouse. Tons of them. Enough porn for an entire village in the mid-west.

Our eyes darted up and down the street and back to the Richards house as we shoved magazines in our shirts. A million thoughts were racing through my head as we committed one of the ultimate acts of preteen crime, possession of nudie magazines. Could I get it back into my room without my parents seeing? Was there somewhere outside I could stash them? I needed time to think. My dad was painting in the house; my mom was in the kitchen. The garage was a good temporary place, but it was in view of the kitchen windows.

I jumped on my bike and went the long way with the stack of magazines clutched under my shirt and against my chest. There was a chance someone else might see me by going the long way but it lowered the risk of my parents seeing me. I was able to get into the garage from the back side instead of right past the kitchen windows.

I managed to get inside without being spotted. I saw the garbage can filled with sand for the driveway in the winter. Perfect. I looked a little closer at what I had as I put them in. Two Hustlers, a Penthouse and two Playboys. I would later learn that Playboy sucked and I should have grabbed more Hustlers, but for now I had to find my older brother. He would have to think I was cool if I had porn right?

I ran into the house. "Jacky, wanna play a game outside," I yelled up the steps, ignoring my mother so that she wouldn't think anything was up. I didn't get any response so I just ran up to his room his door was closed. "Jacky!" I banged on the door.

Chuck Howe

"Go away!" I tried the knob, it was locked.
I lowered my voice so only he could hear
"Jacky, you have to come see..."
"I was already outside, I found it. Go away!"

Miss Dellvecchio

"Here comes Miss Dellvecchio," was the feared phrase in the second grade lunch room. She was rail thin and short, but her hair doubled her height. She always had a mean scowl on her face as she surveyed the cafeteria looking for her next victim. She would see a kid eating his cookie before he finished his sandwich and she would swoop down on him. Her weapons of choice were ten razor sharp, seemingly titanium reinforced fingernails.

"Here comes Miss Dellvecchio," came the whispers as she approached our table. Everyone put down their cookies and picked up their sandwiches and pretended not to notice she was coming. Everyone except for Harry. Harry's back was to her, and he had a huge smile on his face as he bit down on his Chip's Ahoy. We all gasped in horror as we saw her claws rise up in the air, and come down on Harry's shoulder, digging in deep. We expected Harry to cry out in pain, some of us even did it for him, but he just took another slow deliberate bite of cookie.

"Mister Roman, you will put down that cookie right now and finish your sandwich." Harry defiantly took the last bite of his cookie, and then reached in his pocket and handed Miss Dellvecchio a note:

"My son, Harry Roman, is allowed to eat his lunch in

whatever order he chooses.
Signed,
Janet Roman"

Miss Dellvecchio huffed in disgust and walked away with her head hanging low but even more on the lookout for misbehaving than ever. The entire table let out a cheer and we all ate our cookies before we finished our sandwiches. She never bothered us again about the order we ate our lunch, instead she became the leader of the noise police. Children made too much noise, especially at lunch, when they should be eating sandwiches. She would put a stop to that.

A few weeks later we were lining up to march back into our classroom after recess. Again, this was Miss Dellvecchio's job. I was never considered the quietest child in the class, but for some reason she decided that was the day she would crack down on my crime of being loud.

"Mister Howe, since you are so eager to make noise, why don't you just stay out here and you can make all the noise you want, while I take the rest of the students back to class." She had a point. I was pretty damn eager to make some noise, and I took it as, "Hey Chuck, make as much noise as you want for a little while." I had never known her to reward a student before, but here she was letting me stay outside and make noise, while the rest of the kids had to go back to class. Of course I took her up on the offer. The second she was in the door I started singing, at the top of my lungs, the hit song of the day.

"Whatsa matter you, HEY! Gotta no respect, Hey! Whatta you think you do, Hey! Why you looka sad, HEY! Itsa not so bad, Itsa nice a place, Ah Shut uppa you face!" I just sang it over and over. Of course I was on the steps leading to the front door, and the principal's office was right next to the front door. It only took about three times through the chorus before the Principal was at the door.

"Chuck! What the Hell are you doing?" He asked in his big loud principal voice. "Miss Dellvecchio told me to do it."

Charlie Hustle

Baseball was always one of those games that I loved to watch and talk about and dissect. I could tell at a young age that Pete Rose was a competitor. Pete Rose ran to first base every time he walked. Pete Rose slid head first into the bag. Pete Rose was the hard working everyman. Pete Rose was Charlie Hustle. I wanted to be that kind of ball player. My name was Chuck, but I wanted to become Charlie Hustle. My brother was two years older and was the star pitcher of his little league team. I could get lots of hits off him playing wiffle ball in the back yard, and if he was a good pitcher, I must be a great hitter.

Finally the day came where I got to try out for little league. First I got to watch my classmates Harry and Butch. They were both great. Of course they were both big and tough, even in 5th grade. Next it was my turn. Unlike Butch and Harry, I wasn't big and tough.

First I had to show what I could do in the field. They put me at second base and hit a grounder to me. I moved to the ball, just like I had practiced, and put my glove down. The ball hopped right over my glove and hit me in the chest. It hurt a lot more than a wiffle ball. I scooped the ball up and tried to throw to first. It wasn't even close to the First-baseman. They hit a few more to me, and the same thing happened every time.

It was with great relief that I was told to get a bat and helmet and warm up. I was on deck. This was perfect. Hitting was my specialty. I could even hit Jacky's wiffle curve. But I was a small kid and even the smallest helmet was way too big for me, the brim kept flopping around as I tried my warm up swings. I had a weight at the end of the bat, just like I saw the pros do, but I could barely control it as I tried swinging it around. Finally it was my turn. I tightened my brand new batting gloves and knocked the dirt out of my cleats. I dug into the batter's box and nodded to the pitcher telling him I was ready. Nodding of course made the helmet shift which completely covered my eyes. Pop. I heard the ball hit the mitt; I didn't know what else to do so I swung.

Chuck Howe

The coach waited for me to adjust my helmet and then threw another pitch. This time I saw it and swung at the right time but I swung the bat about a foot over the ball. I kept swinging and missing until I finally lucked out and connected. The ball dribbled weakly in foul territory down toward first base. "Next." called the coach.

Luck, and the fact that my father was going to be the coach of the Elks Club team that year, were on my side. My father came home from draft night and to everyone's surprise, he was able to draft me. The bidding must have been intense. I never really got much better, but by the end of my little league days I had two things down perfectly. One was the angry look at the ump after a called strike three, but having a very small strike zone, I walked a lot. The other thing I had down was that every time I walked, I would run full speed to first base because I was Charlie Hustle.

Puppy Love

In fifth grade I was picked to do an extracurricular after school program at the Middle School. There were three other elementary schools in our district, and I would be meeting a bunch of those kids before we were all put in middle school together in 6th grade. There were several choices as to what we could do. I picked "Project Adventure," a ropes course in the woods that was meant to help team building skills.

It was only a weekly thing, so it took a few weeks to really meet any of the kids from the other schools, but one girl caught my eye the first day. It was Kimmy Ross. Kimmy was the girl that would break a million hearts through the next seven years of school and was just starting to realize it. For the next few weeks I made sure I was always on her team for our projects. It worked; we talked a lot and worked well together. Finally I asked her if she would be my girlfriend.

She said no. She was too young to have a boyfriend. So I asked again the next week. Again she said no. I kept asking and she kept saying no. We discovered that we were both going to the same day camp that summer. The next week I asked her and she finally agreed. I had a girlfriend from another school.

Of course none of my friends at Mt. Kisco Elementary believed me. Kimmy and I were doing nothing different. I don't even think I called her once the first few weeks. I was in 5th grade; a girlfriend was an abstract concept.

"Did you kiss her yet?" asked Butch.

"No."

"Did you go on a date yet?" asked Harry.

"No."

"Then how do you know she's your girlfriend?" they both asked together.

"Because she said so."

"Yeah right. Hey everyone! Chuck has a Fake Girlfriend from another school," Butch ran down the hall singing.

A few weeks later there was a concert during school of all of the different Orchestras and Choruses from the four different schools.

Chuck Howe

Kimmy was in the chorus from her school. I sat in the audience waiting for her to come out. Finally her class came walking out on stage. I was sitting with all of my doubting classmates. I stood up and furiously waved to her. She gave a small little shy wave back.

"Holy shit! Chuck does have a girlfriend from another school," Butch yelled out, my amazed friends all cheered and Kimmy's face turned bright red on stage. We continued being boyfriend and girlfriend into the summer, although still not actually dating or anything. Finally we had a big camp trip to Playland Amusement Park. I kind of thought it would be like an actual date. We could hang out all day and go on the roller coaster and be all grown up romantic all day. I don't think I ever told Kimmy that was my plan, or maybe I did, and it scared her and that's why things turned out the way they did.

I got on the bus all excited, telling my friends to stay out of my seat. It would be for Kimmy. The bus began filling up and I kept telling people I was saving the seat for Kimmy. Finally, her friend Emily sat down.

I told her I was saving it. "That's OK," she said, "I'll only be a second. So, ummm, let me ask you something. Would you like, dive in front of a truck to save Kimmy?"

I figured it was a test or something, so I immediately jumped in, "Of course I would!"

"Well maybe you shouldn't, because Kimmy wants to break up with you." She got up and walked away and I sat there with my jaw on the ground. I was heartbroken. Instead of Kimmy, I sat next to Butch on the rollercoaster. Nowhere near as romantic as I had planned. I sulked around for the rest of the summer, completely inconsolable.

In the fall I went to the Middle School. Suddenly there were beautiful girls from three other schools all around me. Although I didn't completely forget about Kimmy, there was more than enough to distract me and pull me out of my sorrow.

I quickly joined the cool kids dating carousel, which every now and then would end up matching me with Kimmy again. She would be my first kiss and we would even get married at one point outside on a hill next to the school. We even had funky orange neon rubber rings.

If I Had Wings These Windmills Would Be Dead

The marriage didn't last, and a few months later we would find ourselves dating again. By this point we had gotten much better at the dating thing. We went to see Footloose about 4 times, mostly because it played in the theater for about 6 months. At one point I tried to stick my hand up her shirt. She pushed me away. She claimed she didn't have tits yet, I claimed not to care, but gave up.

A few summers later, we found ourselves on a weeklong camping trip near Chautauqua, a gated musical community. During a game of truth or dare, I got to stick my tongue down her throat, and before we knew it we were dating again. One of the greatest moments of our dating career happened when she told me she needed to run in to the Chautauqua Library. It seemed odd to me, it was summer, why go to a library?

Right before we walked in, she took a scarf and wrapped it around her head. She put on a pair of giant sunglasses and put on way too much bright red lipstick. She looked ridiculous, like a 14 year old girl trying to look like an old gypsy woman. I should have known her well enough to know something was up, but I naively went inside with her.

She walked up to the front desk and in a very straight laced, quiet voice asked, "Do you have any books on poltergeists?"

"Excuse me?" The librarian asked, with a startled expression.

"Poltergeists," Kimmy said a little louder. "Do you have any books on poltergeists?" She almost yelled. The woman began to answer but Kimmy fell straight to the floor motionless. I had no idea what the hell was going on, so I was just looking down at her in shock. A woman who just happened to be standing nearby came running over, bent down and began lifting up Kimmy's head. Kimmy couldn't hold it in any more and started giggling. The woman, shocked just dropped her head and it slammed against the floor. This actually caused Kimmy to start laughing as hard as I have ever seen her. That caused me to start cracking up. The librarian got super pissed and actually chased us out of the library.

At the end of the week she told me she wanted to go back to the library and apologize. Of course I believed her and went. We walked up to the front desk, but instead of an apology, Kimmy asked, "Do you have any books on kleptomania?" as her hand slowly grabbed the librarian's stapler and brought it to her purse"

Cobra vs. Mongoose

I first met Bob Afetti in the library when we were both supposed to be in gym class. We both fabricated some injury to get out of sweating at school. We were supposed to study or do homework or some boring shit like that in the library. I spent most of my first day of freedom checking out the nudes in the classic art books. The second day I found Bob sitting at one of the cart video machines.

I didn't really know Bob at all. He went to a different elementary school, and I had no classes with him. He was a pretty big kid, but most kids were, compared to me. He always seemed really angry, and liked punching kids. That didn't really scare me. My friend Butch in elementary school had been known as a bully. I got along great with him, so I felt like I could get along with Bob, too. It turned out that he wasn't really a bully. He just liked punching shit, sometimes people. Once, on a trip to Colorado with a bunch of our friends, he was seen recklessly flying down the mountain, completely out of control. The nickname Ada Con stuck from then on.

The carts were big plastic cartridges that had 30 or 60 seconds worth of film in them. As I walked by Bob grabbed my arm. "Check this shit out." He put a cart in the machine, and a black and white video came on.

It was called "Cobra vs. Mongoose," and sure enough 60 seconds of a mongoose and snake fighting followed. It was a pretty fair fight, but the mongoose won at the very end. Bob and I were cheering at top volume.

The librarian hushed us and Bob grabbed me and brought me to where hundreds of carts were stored. I looked down the list of name. Hawk vs. Python. Alligator vs. Cougar. Dog vs. Tail. Then there were things like Sherman Tank vs. Tiger Tank, Blitzkrieg and D-Day. War and animals fighting. It was prepubescent heaven.

"This is the best gym class ever," Said Bob. And it was.

The Piss Test

When I was in second grade I had bladder surgery and was in the hospital for two weeks. At a follow up doctor's appointment, I was told to always use the bathroom, right away, as soon as I felt the urge. I assumed he meant for a while until the stitches all healed, but I remembered what he said. Two years later I was bored in class and asked to use the bathroom. The teacher at first said no, I had been to the bathroom once already that day. I waited a minute and then asked again. I was told no, and suddenly a light went on.

"But I had bladder surgery and was told to go whenever I had too." It was the same teacher that I had in second grade and she remembered, so she let me go. In fifth grade I told the teacher right away about my bladder surgery, now three years past, and how the doctor told me to always use the bathroom as soon as I felt the need. The teacher seemed skeptical, so I tried to be apologetic ahead of time. I'm sure that she asked my mother about it at the parent/teacher conference, and I'm sure my mother said yes, the doctor did tell me that, because he did. From then on I had almost free range of the hallways during class.

Then I got to the sixth grade, a new school and different teachers in every class. I figured I could get away with getting out of every class for at least five minutes. It would be great. I wasn't the only one who thought this way, obviously, and pretty soon the teachers started getting upset that we were all going to the bathroom so much. It really bothered the science teacher, Mrs. Nordstrom.

At first she kept a bathroom log in her classroom. I just didn't go to the bathroom that much in her class so I was below her radar, but then she got all of the other teachers in on it. Suddenly you had to sign out to use the bathroom in every class. After the first week, I was called into the office. Mrs. Nordstrom stood there with the sign out sheets from the last week.

"Four times Monday. Five times Tuesday. Three times Wednesday. Five times Thursday and six times Friday. What do you have to say for yourself?"

"I had bladder surgery and the doctor told me to use the bathroom as soon as I felt like I needed to." I gave her a smug look I am sure she didn't like.

"Six times on Friday?" she yelled out angrily. "That's almost every class. We will see about this." It was the days before computers were everywhere, so she went to a rolodex in the office and found my card. She found my mother's number at work and dialed the phone, almost punching at the numbers.

"Hello Mrs. Howe? This is Mrs. Nordstrom, your son's science teacher. Yes. I am here with your son because he seems to be using the bathroom too often. Um. Yes. Yeah. Um yeah, he told us he had bladder surgery but... Umm. OK. Sure. I'm sorry. Good bye." She gave me a murderous look. She knew I was fucking around during class. She had the proof right there and there was nothing she could do. "Get back to class." She said quietly.

"I would like an apology first," I said with a completely straight face. I had won, and I wanted to make sure she knew it. She said nothing. I walked out of the office singing Pink Floyd's "Another Brick in The Wall."

The next day in her class, I waited for Mrs. Nordstrom to take attendance. Right as she started her lesson I asked to use the bathroom. She never actually said yes, she just grunted. I made a grand gesture of signing the bathroom log. I slowly walked to the door and made my way down the hall. I got a drink at the water fountain on the way. Read the fliers on the wall and finally made my way to the bathroom. Steve was in there. We talked for a few minutes. He went back to class. I washed my hands, and then finally peed, after standing there for two minutes because I didn't have to piss at all.

I washed my hands again and slowly made my way out of the bathroom. I got another drink at the water fountain. Mmm, it was good water. I had some more. When I finally felt like I had been gone long enough, I made my way back to class. I slowly opened the door and walked in. I slowly closed the door behind me, pretending I didn't want it to make any noise, and then slinked back to my seat. It was a full fifteen minute piss break. The whole class expected Mrs. Nordstrom to freak out. She just turned and continued her lesson. Soon enough, the bathroom logs disappeared.

Pyrotechnics

With the cigarette held up by the tension of my thumb and middle finger, I lined up my shot. I released and the burning cigarette went flying. It arced across the small stream and went right into the hole in the tree on the other side.

"You owe me a million bucks Rawley." We laughed, picked up our BB Guns and started to make our way out of the woods back toward my house. Rawley was a few years younger than me, but I never had a younger brother and he filled in nicely. His father played bass for Expatriate, an extremely popular band from England. Their last few albums had gone to the top of the charts. But Rawley seemed as interested in my middle class family as I was in his globetrotting musician father. He loved helping me help my father building shit around the house. He got as much joy in it as I got from having a Top Ten musician make me a grilled cheese sandwich.

The next morning I woke up to a beautiful spring day. My bedroom window faced out to my beloved woods and the first thing I did was throw open the window to breathe in the fresh morning air. It must have been really cold in the morning because it smelled like someone had their fireplace roaring. I grabbed my BB gun and my cigarettes, told my parents I'd be back in a few and made my way into the woods. As I got close to my usual spot it dawned on me that the nice fireplace smell wasn't coming from a neighbor: it got stronger the further into the woods I went. As I got close to the stream, I could see smoke rising out of the top of the tree with a hole in it.

I panicked and ran to it. Sure enough the hole now stretched to the ground. The fire had travelled up the trunk. The only thing holding the tree up was the bark and charred outermost layer of wood. I freaked out and ran to get Rawley. When I told Rawley he started freaking out too. We went back to my house and grabbed two buckets and went back out into the woods. By the time we got back to the tree there were other neighborhood kids checking it out. When they saw us coming, they scattered.

We got to work. Luckily the tree was right at the side of the stream. We kept trying to throw buckets of water up the hole. It really wasn't working. The neighborhood kids did a good enough job of spreading the story around and soon enough I looked up to see my father with a Rock star holding a chainsaw walking up the trail.

My dad figured out where to cut the tree so it would land where we wanted it too, and Rawley's dad started cutting. It fell perfectly. We cut it into sections and dumped water on each section until we were sure it was out. At one point my dad asked me how it started and I said I didn't know. He pointed to a crumpled pack of smokes that I must have one day thrown at the hole and missed. "I do."

Once we were sure everything was out we started hiking back through the woods. My dad, Rawley, a rock star and me. Covered in soot, we looked like the cast of the worst afterschool special starring a pop star ever.

Battlefield Bedford

It was Halloween night. I was dressed as a kid in an Army jacket with pockets full of fireworks, shaving cream and eggs. I had a foot long metal tube in my right sleeve. In theory, I could launch bottle rockets out of the tube, my own never tested improv bazooka. My friends and I were all set to invade Hoyt Road.

We started off actually trick or treating. We needed to build up a nice sugar rush for the mayhem to come. Soon enough we came across the first group of kids we knew from school. We sprayed some shaving cream and threw a couple of eggs, but both groups were saving their ammo. After a quick skirmish, we made peace and decided to team up and ambush the next group of kids we saw.

When the next group of kids came by the curve, we launched our attack. I could see one was Steve, one of my best friends. So I hit him in the chest with an egg before our groups made peace, and we became a gang.

We started our random destruction rampage. Pumpkins were smashed, mailboxes filled with shaving cream, one blown up by an M-80 of course. We were busy TP-ing a tree, so no one noticed the windowless van pull up. Suddenly the doors on the side swung open and three masked kids with BB guns started their rampage. We took off running across the yard as they fired on us.

A few of us had been involved in BB gun wars the year before. We knew they hurt; Steve had to get a BB taken out of his scalp after what turned out to be our final war. We tried to get away by running to the neighboring yard. There seemed to be more cover next door.

None of us saw the chicken-wire fence between the two yards and it was as if someone punched those of us in the lead in the stomach all at the same time. I flipped over the fence landing on the tube in my arm. This was it. This was my big chance.

I pulled out an 8 ounce rocket. A big one. One that made a big sparkly explosion. I placed it in the tube, pointed it at the van, lit the fuse and turned my head. ZIIIIIIP I heard it fire off. I looked, my sleeve wasn't on fire and the rocket was headed right for the open doors of the van. It went right inside and flared up. The van immediately sped away with the kids inside all yelling and screaming.

I walked to the neighbor's house, knocked on the door and said, "Trick or Treat." It was the best tasting Kit Kat ever.

MACHETE

It was a typical summer day for 14 year old Chuck. I had worked from 7-3 at the tennis club and when I got home I went right into the woods. Most days I would bring my dog and my gun and maybe take out a squirrel. There were deer all over, but I didn't think it was sporting to shoot a deer in your own woods. Squirrels were tough to hit, especially from a distance, and there were tons of them around. I rarely got one, and when I did, the dog would run and fetch it like a good golden retriever will do.

I had named the dog Honey because I was always the first one home from school or work every day. It was nice to walk in and say "Honey, I'm home," and be greeted by a smiling face. This day she was upset when I got her collar. That meant we were going for a walk on the street and not the woods. I had a mission in the woods that day.

There was an old foundation on top of a hill, overlooking the stream that split the woods. It was the perfect impenetrable base for a BB gun or paint ball war. There were a bunch of trees and weeds growing inside it. I was planning on clearing it out in hopes of building it into a clubhouse in the woods. So instead of the gun, I made my way into the woods with my machete.

It took about ten minutes to walk back through a narrow deer trail that had been cleared even more by my daily treks. I was practicing my swing on every branch and vine I could as I made my way back to the foundation. The trees growing inside the foundation were pretty small, but armed with just the machete, it took awhile to cut them down. I was getting pretty tired, and about to call it a day. My mom would be home from work, and she might have even gone grocery shopping, so I was getting eager to start heading back. There was one last low lying branch coming into the foundation from a tree outside of it. I did a test swing, and the branch was pretty solid. I was going to have to give this one a bunch of whacks before it came down. I gave it a pretty hard downward whack and the blade went about halfway through. I thought one good whack and it will probably come down.

I pulled the machete back and gave it a really hard overhead swing.

Chuck Howe

The machete sliced through the branch like butter, it was a good clean hit. Unfortunately I was expecting a little more resistance so my follow through left me off balance. BANG. It felt like I had just banged my knee hard against something. My hand immediately went down to the spot and my finger slipped inside the cut and I was touching the bone. I looked down. The side of my knee was sliced open.

Shit. I was far in the woods. I was bleeding, but not as bad as I would have thought. I took off my t-shirt and tied it loosely around my knee. I grabbed one of the small trees I had just cut down, and used the machete to make it a decent walking stick length and began to make my way back to the house. The first part, going downhill from the foundation, was the hardest part. It may only take 10 minutes to walk in, but it took me at least a half hour to hop back to the house.

As I emerged from the woods in the back of my yard, I could see my mom's car. It was good she was home from work, she could drive me to the hospital for stitches, but it was bad because she didn't exactly know that I owned a machete. I didn't really hide it. I kept it in the garage mixed in with the pile of wiffleball bats, golf clubs, hockey sticks and lacrosse sticks. Hey, my brother had his sports, I had mine. The only problem was now I had to tell my mom what happened. There really was no way to bullshit my way out of this one. As I got close to the house, I could hear her through the open kitchen window.

"Mom?" I called out in my best innocent little boy voice.

"Yes, Chuck?" She called sweetly from inside the house.

"Can we go somewhere?" I asked very politely, as if that would

keep her from yelling in five seconds.

"Where do you want to go, Chuck?"

"To the Hospital..." She looked out of the window and saw me leaning against the car, shirtless. Blood drenched shirt wrapped around my knee, machete still in my hand.

"What the hell did you do?!? Are you OK? Where the hell did you get a machete?!? Can you walk? You are such an idiot! Here take off that shirt, here are some paper towels. You could have cut your damned leg off!!! Here buckle up. How did I raise such a moron! Does it hurt? Don't worry we'll be there soon ..."

Buses and Blunts

The bus drivers were always stoned. That's the way it was in the 80's. You got on the school bus with the understanding that the bus driver was high. It wasn't just my bus, it was all of them. At the end of each school day, 20 stoned men and women waited to launch their giant yellow missiles full of screaming kids.

On one particular Friday, I couldn't wait to get home. That night 4 friends and I would be taking a limo to the Pink Floyd concert at Giants Stadium. I took my spot on the bus in the back seat, like the good Hooligan leader that I was. It was a quiet day. There were no fights brewing on the bus. I wasn't even looking for a female mouth to stick my tongue in. I was actually almost well behaved, just getting excited for the concert.

The first kid our bus dropped off was pretty much right outside of the school on a main road. We stopped. The kid got up and was making his way to the front when I looked out the back window. There was another bus coming up. It was coming fast. I could see the bus driver in the window. He was looking in his rear view mirror and yelling at kids, not paying any attention to the road.

"This might hurt a bit," I thought as the other bus got closer and closer. I kept hoping the bus driver would see us and slam on the brakes, but it didn't happen until right before he got to us. A quick squeal of brakes was cut off by the loud bang of the bus hitting us. I was sure I was going to end up in the grill. I shut my eyes and covered my head.

Glass shattered. The metal of the bus pushed up into the back of my seat, but stopped right before ripping through it. Other than being thrown forward a little, the big impact I was expecting never came. I opened my eyes to see the other bus driver, now only about a foot away from me, with only twisted steel and broken glass between us.

Our bus driver came running back to make sure we were all OK. He started talking about getting everyone checked out by the school before we could go home. A vision of the limo leaving for Pink Floyd without me flashed in my head. I couldn't let that happen.

He moved the bus up just a little so the bus that hit us could be looked at. The kids on that bus would need to get on another to be taken back to school. When the buses disconnected, the back emergency door pulled open.

"OK, we are heading back to school," the bus driver called out. I looked at the broken safety door falling off of its hinges. I was fine. I didn't need to miss a concert to have the school doctor to tell me that. The policemen and the bus drivers were just finishing up talking about what happened. They were distracted. I pushed on the back door. It opened a little more, just enough for me to get out.

I crawled out. No one saw. I ran along the side of the bus where the driver and police couldn't see me. After getting away from the scene, I stuck my thumb out hoping for a safer ride home. There was no way getting hit by a bus would keep me from Pink Floyd.

The Swing's Revenge

I was looking at her when it happened. Kelly was sitting on the swing, one of those handmade swings, just a board and two ropes. She wasn't even swinging, just sitting there. She leaned back just a little and... Flip. Bam. She flipped backwards off the swing onto her head. I ran over worried, but could tell she was laughing before I even got to her.

I helped her get up and she seemed fine. Almost as a joke I held up two fingers. "How many fingers do I have up?"

"Two," she said groggily. "What happened?"

"I don't know, you just kind of flipped over." She seemed a little out of it so just to make sure she was OK I asked a few simple questions. When was her birthday, what were her parents' names, and where we went to school. One of our friends had just bought a brand new red Jeep Cherokee after crashing his powder blue Subaru a week earlier.

"What color is Will's car?"

"Blue."

"No, his new car."

"Will got a new car? What happened to the Subaru?" Now I was worried.

"He got into an accident..."

"Oh my god is he OK?"

"He's fine." I was already getting ready to take her to the hospital.

"Oh my god, you cut your hair!" She screamed. She had been with me at the barber shop when I had it cut; we had already had this argument.

"Get in the car; we're going to the hospital."

"Why, are you not feeling well?"

Frisbee

Steve and I were throwing a Frisbee around in Kelly's backyard. Kelly's place was the perfect place to hang out after school. Her father had a pool table out in the garage. There was a nice lawn and her parents were very cool. Every time I would go to pick Kelly up for a date, her father would offer me a beer. I was seventeen and about to drive his daughter all over the place. He was Canadian, and didn't think twice about it, so usually I took him up on it.

Rick, the father, was a fun guy. They had a house up in Vermont and he would ski every weekend in the winter. In the summer he would be out windsurfing all the time. He was over fifty, older than my parents, yet seemed more like a teenager than even his daughter did.

Right behind the back yard was swampland, lots of it. Once Kelly had found a turtle walking across her backyard. She put some chicken wire around it while it was walking, and suddenly declared she had a pet turtle. While playing Frisbee, we tried not to hit the turtle.

Steve wasn't the best Frisbee thrower around. Most of his throws came up really short. Every now and then I would have to chase them down, some even going out into the swampy area. There was a trail that cut through the swamp I had never noticed before and at one point the Frisbee went flying down the trail, when I went to get it, I noticed there was a clearing with something in it right down the trail. I walked to see what it was, and to my surprise, I found a tombstone with what looked like a neatly manicured grave in front of it.

Rick Newton
January 16, 1939 – January 15, 1989
Do not mourn for Rick, He was an Asshole

Rick Newton? Kelly's father? That was his birthday. It was his tombstone and it said he had been dead for two years!

"Kelly, Kelly, Kelly!" I ran back to her yard.

"What?"

"Come here!"

I brought her back to the tombstone and she laughed. "Yeah, my father's friends all though he was too old, so they bought him a tombstone for his birthday. It's creepy though; he comes back here and actually cuts the grass and takes care of it."

"Well, not too many people can make sure their own grave is kept clean," I answered.

Authority Song

There are two types of authority one can express. There are many ways to express each, and the two are not mutually exclusive. The first is Earned Authority. There are many ways to earn it, knowledge in a particular subject matter, a history of fairness, or showing true leadership under stress to name a few. History is filled with men and women of Earned Authority.

The second authority is called Chicken Shit in the military, and it's just that. Every six months a general somewhere decides the troops are slacking off on regulations. So they start busting the balls of the officers, who start busting the balls of the soldiers. Chicken Shit keeps rolling downhill. Unfortunately history is filled with Chicken Shit, too. I was discussing this with Bob, and the oddest thing happened. I was explaining it like this:

In high school, I was suspended for yelling at an English teacher, after I asked "Aren't people free to express their own ideas and theories?" and she answered, "Not in my class." I yelled, and maybe used a little harsh language, got up and left class, went to the guidance counselor and asked to be switched into a different English class. The next day the assistant principle pulled me out of a class. The teacher had demanded that I be suspended for one week. I laughed at him. He yelled. I laughed again. I said that I was not going back to the class anyway, so what was the point. He said that "legally" he could only suspend me for one day. I said sure, I wouldn't mind sleeping late any way, left his office laughing at him. The teacher, the assistant principle, neither had ever showed me any reason to show them any respect. Just Chicken Shit.

I went down to see my guidance counselor. She had always shown that she was looking out for the students, so she had some Earned Authority. Unfortunately, because of my science classes, she couldn't get me into another English class. My suggestion was to just drop English, and take it in the summer. I worked full time every summer, but maybe I could change my schedule.

She talked me into trying to go back to class and doing my best. I didn't want to disappoint her so I said I would try. She told me to go get extra work from all of my teachers, so I wouldn't be behind after my suspension. Most of my teachers laughed when I told them. My English teacher was even a bit of a joke among the teachers. As I was telling Bob, there was one teacher who brought me back down to earth. She wasn't angry, she was disappointed. She didn't want to hear why I was suspended. All she said was, "Chuck, you're finally getting a handle on this stuff. You can't afford to miss tomorrow. Come by after school, and I'll go over this stuff real fast. I have to get home early today." My getting suspended was going to put her out. It was the only time I felt bad about what I did.

Bob shocked me by immediately saying, "Ms. Mimno right." She wasn't ever in the running for the most popular teacher, but anyone you asked would say, "She's a good teacher, but she's hard." When talking about a chemistry teacher, hard is not a negative, it's unavoidable. She knew how to get students' attention, and they did well. I realize now more than I did back then what a good teacher she was. Bob used to ask me to drive him home at third period every day, and I thought he'd stay home, but he said, "Yeah, I used to walk through the forest back to school after lunch to go to her class. I'd pick her mushrooms, because if I brought an apple I'd get beaten up. She read me the riot act once when I skipped." She wasn't the "your best buddy" teacher like some at the school. Or the bust your ass for no reason teacher like most at the school. She had earned her authority, and she did it so well, you didn't even know she did it.

Two Weeks

By the end of my junior year in high school, Kelly and I had been dating for a while. I had my driver's license and it would be the first time I ever tried to keep a girlfriend over the summer. She would be going away for a few weeks at the beginning of the summer. It was going to be hell to be apart, but we still had a week or two until she left and it seemed like we were headed for the next phase. I couldn't wait.

During finals week we spent as much time together as possible. Who really needed to study for the next test anyway? Of course the weather was beautiful as it could only be on a June day in New York. Summer was in full swing by the last exam day. We were done by noon, so I planned for Kelly and I to have a little alone time at the reservoir. As the last test of the day ended, I met Kelly at my car; Steve and his girlfriend Lea were with her.

"What are they doing here?" I asked a little too sharply.

Kelly knew exactly what I was planning and gave me a hard look in return.

"I'm sorry stud, but they were hot, too. Since we're going for a swim, I figured you wouldn't mind."

I immediately felt bad. They were good friends and we did pretty much hang out with them everyday anyway. "Umm," I said "it's just that I only have a half bottle of Tequila, and …"

"I think that's plenty," she shot back not buying any of my bullshit. So this wouldn't be the day we entered the next phase, but we would have some fun anyway. So we all jumped in my car and took off for the rope swing on the reservoir.

We had all grown up in the area, and although swimming wasn't allowed in the reservoir, no one had ever stopped us before. But that year there were rumors running rampant that Saddam Hussein was going to try to poison the NYC water supply. All we had in mind was a bottle of Tequila and few jumps off the rope swing into some nice cold water on a hot day. We had to park on a back road and walk a bit into the woods. It wasn't a long walk but as it was hot, the four of us were pretty much stripped down before we even got to the shore. Of course, if you are going to swim in the New York City drinking water supply, the proper etiquette is to do it naked.

Seeing Kelly and Lea both naked made my hormones rage even harder. After Kelly had taken one of her perfect naked ass cannonballs off the swing, I had to swim over and rub on her a bit. She wasn't entirely unreceptive, but pushed me away any time Steve or Lea said a word about anything. They had been dating much longer than we had, and had already entered the next phase. Something that Steve was sure to rub in my face again the next time the girls weren't around.

We had been in the water long enough to finally start cooling off and we were just heading back to the tequila bottle, when all of a sudden we heard a loud voice from the shoreline. "Slowly make your way to the shore with your hands in the air!" I looked up and got that shriveled dick feeling that you can only get when standing naked and someone is pointing a gun at you. It took me a second to realize it was a policeman. "Out of the water! All of you, now!" It was then I noticed he was not only in his full long sleeved dress uniform, but also wearing a bullet proof vest. "Don't try anything funny!"

That just made me start laughing uncontrollably, and that pissed off the cop. "What the hell is so funny?" he yelled, with the gun pointed at my chest. The whole situation was just ridiculous to me. I tried to stay at least somewhat respectful, but even at 16 I could tell that it must be this guy's very first day on the job.

"Sir, can you please put the gun down, obviously we are not carrying any concealed weapons." The four of us were butt naked, just getting out of the water.

"OK, just get dressed. Slowly." He lowered the gun, but still didn't holster it.

"Reverse strip tease?" I couldn't help being a wise ass, but I regretted it as I reached for my clothes and realized the bottle of tequila was under my t-shirt. I put on my boxers and shorts first and waited until he was looking at one of the others to grab my shirt. Somehow it worked. He never actually saw the bottle laying on the ground in broad daylight. Even if he did, I figured I could attempt a "Gee, where could that have come from, it certainly isn't ours" defense. But it wasn't needed.

If I Had Wings These Windmills Would Be Dead

He herded us back to the car, still keeping his gun out. Steve and I gave him our ID's, but the girls were both under 16, so they had no ID. He ended up writing Steve and I a ticket for trespassing and letting the girls off with a warning about hanging out with shifty 16 year old boys. As we were leaving, I noticed the only no trespassing sign was on a tree that had fallen over, slightly obscuring the sign. Kelly always had her camera on her, so I asked her to take a picture.

The court date was the night before Kelly went away. I was in the Youth Court program at school and had done some Mock Trial competitions, so even though I was only 16 I knew my way around a court room. I brought Kelly's picture of the "obscured" no trespassing sign and Steve and I had our charges dropped immediately. Kelly was really impressed with the way I handled myself in court. We had talked about when we were finally going to "do it." She had always said she wasn't ready, and she was younger than me. I accepted it, but didn't exactly drop the discussion either.

As I dropped her off that night, we had a long tearful goodbye. Two weeks apart was going to be murder. As she got out of the car she turned back to me and said, "When I come back from vacation, I think I will be ready."

"Ready for what?" I asked. I like to say that I can be really stupid for a smart man, and this was one of those times.

"Ready for the next phase."

"Oh ..." I thought for a second, "Oh! Cool!" I said. As I drove home I realized that this was going to be the worst two weeks of my life. The two weeks dragged on, but eventually she came home. The only problem was she had lost that "I'm ready" feeling and I needed to work hard to bring it back.

"Soon, two weeks maybe." She kept saying. Three months later, the longest two weeks of my life were finally over.

Yellow Barn

I walked into the type of bar you only went to if you were depressed, or were under 21; the bouncers at all the other bars knew your brother, and you had his ID. On the day Kelly told me she had a new boyfriend, I was both. We were still very much in love when I left for school, but we had agreed to see other people. The reality didn't hit until she actually found someone. She was still in high school, I was in college, I was supposed to find someone first.

The bar seemed dark and almost empty when I first walked in. There were two old fucks crying in their beers. They would be perfect company. The place had darts, a game on the TV, a jar of pickled hard boiled eggs and that was it. But I glanced down to the end of the bar and was immediately caught up in Michelle's giant brown eyes instead. They were staring a hole right through me. I froze. She turned on her barstool still looking right into my eyes and pulled the stool next to her out, the most inviting move a women has ever made toward me.

A few hours later it was either love or the inability to stand up straight that saw us walking home arms wrapped around each other. Everything about this girl was perfect. It was the fall of 1991 and all the kids were just starting to get into grunge music. She liked the Dead. She was Canadian and she liked hockey. She had a beautiful laugh and best of all, she was into me. Everything screamed out for me to kiss her as we got to her dorm. As I moved in she turned her head and I got nothing but cheek. "I want to, but not yet. Call me tomorrow." Somehow, even with no real kiss good night, I floated back to my dorm.

Over the next few weeks we spent almost every free moment with each other. She had friends in Ithaca, which wasn't far, so we went there almost every weekend. On one trip back, we pulled over at a yellow barn. We were in the middle of nowhere and chances were no other cars would pass all night, so we decided to investigate the creepy old place.

A rusted hinge that held a padlock had already been ripped from the wood and dangled from the door. As we went inside we heard animals scurry away, a big hole in the roof let in the moon, giving it the perfect mood lighting. I thought this would be it. She still hadn't let me even give her a real kiss. It had only been a short time, but we were in college: shouldn't we have jumped into bed right away?

We lay down under the hole in the roof to watch the stars in each other's arms. I tried to make a few moves, but was politely blocked each time. I got the idea, and just lay there with her. By the time we got up the sun was shining and we had told each other almost every story we had. When we got back to the car I was feeling great, like I had made a real connection.

A week later on that same stretch of road she seemed very distant.

As we approached the yellow barn I pulled over. She looked at me a bit confused, I motioned for us to go and she just shook her head, a small tear coming out of her large brown eye. "Come on," I said, "You can tell me inside." I couldn't imagine what was wrong. Things seemed to be going so well, right up until we left for Ithaca that Friday. She slowly got out of the car and made her way to the barn.

We just lay there in the quiet for what seemed like an eternity. The moon wasn't as full, so it was darker inside. Clouds covered the sky exposed by the hole. She lifted her head up on her elbow and looked right at me. There was a deep sadness in her eye, but for a second I thought she was going to kiss me.

"I went to the bar that night to get drunk and forget all about love. Then you walked in the door." I started to speak, but she stopped me, "just let me get through this. Scott had called that day." She had told me all about him. He was a lazy asshole from what I could gather. "He told me he that he had been a junkie for the last year. I never knew. He found out last month that he is HIV positive." My heart stopped beating. AIDS had been around a few years but still so little was known about it, especially by an 18 year old kid. "I was tested two weeks ago…"

She buried her face deep in my chest and I could feel her body shaking with the spasms of her tears. I just looked up at the blank hole in the ceiling. I tried to think of something to say, but nothing came so I just held her tight. I was afraid I might break a bone, hers or mine. She made strange noises as she muffled her cries with my body. Her face was completely lost inside me.

I looked down at her in the dark. I tried to stop myself but a single laugh escaped. Her head immediately jerked up. Her large, beautiful brown bloodshot eyes looked at me through tears. She was confused. She tried to say something but words wouldn't come.

"I'm sorry, for a second there you looked like a lioness feeding on my ripped open heart," I said.

Her look of confusion turned into a small smile. She gave me a quick eye roll and the smile faded, but it was the most beautiful smile I had ever seen. She put her head down and went back to feeding without another word until the black hole in the ceiling began to turn gray.

CRASH OF '91

I had just spent a semester in hell at the completely wrong school for me. I figured I would live at home, take a few classes at the local SUNY and look at a few schools on the west coast for the fall. I went back to my high school, to meet with my old guidance counselor. She had told me to go to Hampshire College the year before, which probably would have been a much better choice. She seemed to be a pretty bright woman, so I figured I'd run my plan past her when I went to get my transcript sent to SUNY. I knocked on the door to her office; she was alone, but on the phone. She motioned for me to sit down.

"OK, something may have just come up, I'll let you know," she said, then hung up the phone and took a long hard look at me. "So where is your girlfriend? She didn't show up for school. That was her mom."

She wasn't my girlfriend anymore, but I knew she meant Kelly. She was still in high school and I guess she had become quite the troublemaker since I left. "Umm, I don't know actually. I came to ask you about schools out west."

"Chuck I would love to talk with you, but I have no time today. Your girlfriend is missing, and Aaron Cass died in a car accident this morning. He has three sisters in this school. Make an appointment with the secretary." She shooed me away and picked up the phone, but she had just dropped a bombshell on me.

I had known Aaron since the First Grade. He had graduated with me the year before. He lived right down the street from me and we used to play after school. He was debugging computer programs for IBM in the late seventies and early eighties, before he was ten years old. Our elementary school had an Aaron Cass Day when he won our district a whole bunch of computers in some computer contest.

The kid was an absolute genius. I tied him on a spelling test in second grade and I still remember it, that's how much of a genius he was. He missed ONE question on the SAT test. That's right he missed one, and a math one to boot. So what did Aaron do? He got the SAT board to admit that using a different equation, the answer that Aaron gave was in fact a correct answer.

Chuck Howe

Poor Aaron was the classical 80's nerd. He had the glasses that were taped in the middle, the retainer, and the pocket protector, but he embraced the image as his own and was very comfortable with it. He went through a long period where he only wore blue. Blue shirts and blue pants. Everyday blue.

Poor Aaron should have been a millionaire. He shouldn't have had to work every morning so that he could afford to live at school. He shouldn't have been the one in the other lane when that woman hit the patch of ice. The woman was fine. Aaron died of smoke inhalation. The world is fucked up like that.

I didn't make an appointment. I was done with this place. I knew where Kelly was, but I wasn't going to say anything. I couldn't blame her for not wanting to come to this place. I just hoped she didn't smoke all of my pot, cause I needed a bong hit after that morning.

Ballroom Gin

It started off like any other Phish Concert. A mysterious gray-bearded man wearing matching tie dyed button down shirt and pants walked up to me and said "look at my ring." He held out his fist and he had a big red ruby ring in an antique gold setting. "Hold out your hand." I did as he asked and he opened his fist, dropping a small square of paper in my hand.

I immediately put it on my tongue. "Thank you," I said with joy.

"Enjoy the show," replied Gandalf the Tie Dyed and he disappeared on the wind. I turned and walked inside.

They were playing in the Roseland Ballroom in the heart of New York City. Many great acts have played there, and now I was going to see my four favorite music geeks from Vermont melt the dance floor. By the third or fourth song the paper was starting to kick in. My mindscape was being painted with the brush strokes of the artists on stage. I was lost in a piano solo when I felt a tugging on my arm.

"Come with me to get a drink." It was my friend Steve. I looked, the bar was far away. Almost as far away as my mind was.

"No man, that's far."

"Come with me man. I'll buy you a drink." 18 years old in a club in New York City, hell yeah I'd take a free drink. So we made our way through an ocean of dancing freaks. Even in my haze I kept track of where we were coming from. Our ride was still back with our group of friends, and at that point I had no idea where the car was. Steve made his way up to the bar and I was right behind him. I heard him ask for two gin and tonics and I turned to watch the band while the bartender mixed them up. I wasn't a huge fan of gin, but it was alcohol and it was free. I wasn't going to complain.

I was beginning to get lost in the music again when Steve put the drink in front of my face. As I grabbed it, I could hear the bartender ask for 16 dollars. 16 dollars was a hell of a lot of money for two drinks. Steve just looked at me and said, "Run!"

I took off. I weaved in and out of the line of people waiting to get up to the bar. I could hear Steve right behind me. I got to where the dance floor started, and it seemed like I was blocked by people. I stopped for a split second. I saw two groups of people passing each other and had just a split second to get between them. I heard someone come up behind me fast and figured it was Steve. Without looking I grabbed his wrist and took off. We both made it between the groups as they closed up behind us, blocking off anyone who might be following. Still wanting to get far from the bar and back to my friends, I let go of the wrist and started back through the crowd. I grew up running around in the woods, so I treated the dancers like I would have the trees and branches. I weaved in and out with a million near collisions. I was still going fast, but more because I couldn't wait to get back to tell everyone how Steve and I got away with two drinks. I couldn't hear him behind me anymore, but I figured once we made it to the dance floor we were safe, and he knew where we were all hanging out.

I got back to my group and was telling the story, expecting Steve to show up any second. Though I wasn't a fan of gin, it was the best tasting, free, 8 dollar gin and tonic I ever had. When the first set ended, there was still no sign of Steve. It wasn't that big a place. I figured he'd find us during the set break, but Phish came back on stage and there was still no Steve.

The show ended and we slowly made our way out of the place. We were all busy talking about the show, comparing highlights, and not even thinking of Steve until we got back to the car. There he was, sitting on the bumper.

"Hey Steve, was that a great show or what?" I joyfully called out.

"I wouldn't know, I got thrown out."

"What? How? When?" At that point I had almost forgotten about the drink episode.

"Right when I said run. The bartender grabbed me before I even took a step."

"That wasn't you right behind me?" I asked in disbelief. I realized I had never actually turned around to see if it was him.

"No man. Some big security guard took off after you. I figured he caught you and you'd be out here with me soon enough."

"So that wasn't you running right behind me almost the whole way?"

"Nope."

"That wasn't your wrist that I grabbed and led through the crowd for a bit?"

He laughed long and hard. "No, not at all. It was probably the security guard."

Call the Dogs

Scooter wanted out of Colgate. The year was over and he was ready to come home. He had already applied to other schools and it looked like he was going to get into Hampshire. I had already decided to head out to the University of Oregon in the fall, so I wouldn't see too much of my friends.

Phish was playing in Syracuse that night, and then at a festival in Amherst the next day. Picking up Scooter on the way to the Syracuse show made perfect sense. We loaded his stuff into my car, and with Lenny and Steve, made our way to the show.

Next thing I knew, it was four in the morning, and I was tripping my balls off. I was driving 95 miles an hour. I had to make it to Amherst by morning, or else we might not get into the show. We had stayed in Syracuse for too long, but I couldn't see the cigarette in my mouth, let alone the road. Phish had blown our minds. We even got to see Mimi Fishman challenge her son to a vacuum-playing contest. I was so out of it, I had no idea who won. So we waited in the parking lot until I came down enough to drive. Of course once we hit the road, I took another tab. I had to stay awake after all.

Everyone but me was asleep in my car when the cop came up behind me. I didn't even notice him until finally he pulled up alongside of me, and ordered me to pull over. "Everyone, crotch your drugs." Lenny woke up to see a cop pointing his flashlight into the window.

"Everyone out of the car," he ordered. He took one look at me and knew that I was fucked up. "How much have you had to drink tonight?"

"Not a drop sir," I was telling the truth. "How much did you have?"

"OK, so you've been smoking pot. I can smell it on you." He had us sit on the side of the road as more police cars pulled up. "We believe that you may be in possession of illegal substances, so we are going to search the car." Normally I would argue the search, but I was still a little too fucked up to think straight.

He was right. Illegal substances covered almost every inch of my car. Luckily there were a lot of backpacks and all of Scooter's crap from school cluttering the car, but there was also an ounce of pot, a sheet of acid, and 2-dozen Valium. Looking through the back of my Volvo station wagon I could see the police lights swirling through the blue plastic of a two-foot bong. I thought that some dip shit upstate cop was about to make the biggest bust of this town's history.

A few kids walking past stopped to see if we needed help. I said no, but asked them to stick around just in case. "Were you guys at the Phish show?"

I guess it was obvious. "Yeah, it kicked ass."

The cops made us empty our pockets, and Steve pulled out a pack of rolling papers. They immediately began searching my car. I could see the cops opening empty packs of cigarettes, and pulling empty beer bottles out of the back seat. I looked at Lenny and Steve, and they had their heads in their hands. They were sure we were going to jail. As I sat there, I remembered the pipe in my visor and the mushrooms in my glove compartment. I figured we were busted, too. Scooter had no clue what was in the car and was talking happily with the kids who stopped by.

Twenty minutes later, the cops were still searching. If they had looked up they would have seen the bong. I knew then and there that they were a bunch of idiots. I was still tripping my face off, but I figured it was time to talk to the cops.

"Excuse me sir," I said standing up and walking to the cop sitting in the driver's seat. He was sifting through the 300 cigarette butts in my ashtray looking for a roach. That was the only spot in my car without anything illegal. "I've been driving all night, and I still have 4 hours to go. Can we finish this up?" I tried to make it seem like I was not worried at all.

"Tell me where the drugs are. Do you want me to call in the dogs?" I knew if they had dogs, they would have been there already.

If I Had Wings These Windmills Would Be Dead

"Sir, I haven't used any drugs. The smell is probably because we were at a concert." The cop looked at the other cops, and then amazed me by telling them they could go.

"Come to my car. I'll write you a speeding ticket, and if you pass the Breathalyzer you can go." I had no problem with that. I hadn't had a thing to drink. I hated mixing the acid with alcohol.

I walked with him back to his car, passing the bong sticking up like a flag pole. Scooter, Lenny and Steve got up and went back into my car. The officer administered the test, and when I passed, handed me a ticket. "Now drive safe. If you get tired, pull over, or have one of your friends drive."

"Yes sir," I said and went back to my car. I opened the door and got in. Lenny handed me the packed bong, and as the cop pulled past me, I blew the smoke out of the window. I started the car and drove off to Amherst. I wasn't going to miss Phish playing a festival with Fishbone and the Beastie Boys after all.

Nantucket

It was getting near the end of summer and I was looking for a quick trip before heading out to school in Oregon. Scooter suggested we go up to Boston, visit his twin brother Skippy and sell some stuff on the street at Cambridge Square. With the money we made, and obviously it would be billions, we would go to Nantucket for the night. Scooter and I made some beaded necklaces and other little hippy trinkets. Both he and Skippy made some cool paper mache' masks, too. We had some good stuff, plus we were performers, so it would be fun no matter what. It was a perfect plan.

We got to Boston in the early evening and we were cooking when Skippy realized he needed something. I offered to go out and get it. The store was right down the road. Four hours later, on the other side of the city, I walked into a CVS to see if I could get directions back. The kid working behind the counter was, oddly enough, someone I went to high school with in New York. He got me back on the right track and an hour later I was back at Skippy's. "Scott Davidson says hi." was all I said when I came in.

The next day we set up early in Cambridge Square. We sold a few bracelets, but made more money passing the hat after Scooter and Skippy did gymnastics routines while I riled up the crowd and made up a story about how they were gymnasts from Eastern Europe, seeking asylum in the US, and needed help.

We were just ready to pack it up when a man who introduced himself as a Harvard Anthropology Professor started asking about the masks. Two of them in particular caught his eye. He offered fifty bucks and Skippy jumped at it. It was a good end to a fun, if not incredibly profitable, day.

The next day Scooter and I bought a big bottle of cheap vodka and took the ferry out to Nantucket. We checked out all the sites and then found a spot on the beach to camp out under the stars for the night. We built a nice fire, cooked some hot dogs and started in on the vodka. We could see another fire down the beach. Every now and then it would flare up a little and we could hear laughing. The next time it happened. I took a huge swig of vodka and spit half of it into the fire, causing it to jump into the air. We could hear cheers from the other fire. We were passing fire balls back and forth with them the rest of the night.

The sun seemed to come up much too early. We were both still drunk and hungry. We walked into town, but nothing was open yet. There was no movement at all on the street. We could see a full shelf of muffins in a closed bakery and they looked great. I tried the door. There was a simple hook latch on the inside and I could see a gap between the door and the frame. I took out my bank card and was easily ably to pop the latch free.

We went into the dark store. "Muffins, 1 dollar" said the sign. We each took two, left five dollars on the counter and made our way back to the beach. We forgot milk, but there was still some vodka left to wash them down.

The Burning of Nag Champa

Laura was a beautiful blond from the mid west, with the perfect hippie vibe and fashion. She always had a stick of Nag Champa burning wherever she went, and a beautiful rainbow of an aura around her. She always seemed to have a sly smile, like she knew even more about the joke than anyone else. Of course I pretty much fell for her the moment I saw her. I was feeling odd and out of place in a new city on the other side of the country. I am sure she was, too, having just moved out to Eugene herself, but I still felt like she was out of my league. That may have been how I eventually got her. I wasn't expecting sex, so I just treated her like a friend. She was really cool; I simply enjoyed spending time with her.

Once her boyfriend from Indiana, Russ, came and moved in with her, I figured all chances were lost. I ended up hooking up with a lesbian who lived in my dorm. She claimed I was the only man she had ever been with, and I believed her, until I heard a guy down the hall telling the exact same story.

After the first term, my roommate and I were looking to move out of the dorms. So were a few others. Laura's place was really too small for her and Russ, not to mention their friend Chris, who had moved out from Indiana too. My friend, Lenny, called from New York, he was looking to move out to Oregon, so we all went out and found a huge 8 bedroom house in the hills. A total of twelve of us, from New York, Indiana, Chicago, and Finland all moved in, half of us having never met any of the others before.

After a month in the house, Laura and Russ broke up. They both still lived in the house, but in different rooms now. I made a couple of halfhearted attempts at flirtation, but still felt like she was out of my league. Something worked because a few days later Lenny came down to our room with a wicked smile on his face.

"You're an asshole dude," he said with a laugh.

"What did I do this time?" I asked looking up from whatever school book I was pretending to read.

"Laura is completely into you, dick," he added the dick just to let me know that I was, in fact, a dick for allowing a girl to be into me.

I immediately threw my book down and ran up the stairs. I took a deep breath to try to regain my cool before knocking on her door. "Come in," her voice floated through the door. I opened it up to find her sitting on the floor with candles and, of course, Nag Champa burning all around her. On the ground in front of her there was a dark piece of cloth with a bunch of tiny oval shaped white stones on it. There were three directly in front of her and she was reading a book.

"I'm sorry, am I interrupting something?" I asked.

"No, come on in. I was just reading my Runes." I gave her a quizzical look as I closed the door behind me and walked into the room. "Have a seat, when I finish reading mine, we'll do yours." I sat across from her as she finished reading. The 1978 Dead show from Cornell was playing in the background. She had it on CD. She had more Dead bootleg CDs than I had tapes. One more reason I thought she was way out of my league. She finished reading and placed her three stones face down with the rest and then mixed them up as if I would know what was what. "These are like Viking tarot cards. Now put your hands on the stones. Feel them all. If you feel really strongly about one, pull it out and turn it over in front of you until you have three stones."

I took it as seriously as a natural born skeptic can. She obviously put some weight into what these stones told her, and she was some sort of mystic goddess, so who knows what these stones really meant. I had to choose carefully.

One of them seemed to give off a little more heat than the others. I chose that one first. The next was a harder choice. I felt no attachment to any of them. Suddenly one felt a little colder than the rest, so I chose that one. The final one I more or less picked at random. They each had strange markings on them and Laura immediately went to her book.

I don't remember exactly what any of them were specifically, but the gist I got from all three was, "Whatever you are thinking about doing, DON'T DO IT!"

If I Had Wings These Windmills Would Be Dead

So of course I leaned over and kissed her. She got up, locked the bedroom door and blew out the candles on her way back to me. She left the Nag Champa to burn.

The next morning, as I sneaked out of her room before anyone else in the house woke up, I felt my mind start to race and cycle. Russ was not only a friend of mine at this point, but he still lived in the house and he still really loved Laura. He was going to find out eventually. It didn't seem like it was going to be a one night only thing, at least I really hoped not. Laura was too beautiful and cool and awesome to let go. I felt like I had to be with her from then on. There was no other choice really.

Russ was a great guy though. He was a country boy with a country twang to his voice. Quick with a joke, he loved to laugh and was pretty much loved by everyone. He was also huge. Not fat, tall, well built and surprisingly light on his feet. One night he used interpretative dance to explain why the Dead's version of "Dancing in the Streets" was such a good tune, a vision that still stays with me today. Russ was a teddy bear, but I really didn't want to see him angry, and he was going to be angry as hell when he found out about us.

Laura was all smiles to me the next day. Russ was there, so she didn't give any obvious signs of affection, but enough to know she was looking for more. That evening she and Russ got into a huge fight. I was sure she told him about us as he went storming out of the house, not talking to anyone else on the way out. I immediately went into her room. She closed and locked the door and started crying.

She had told Russ that they were over. She hadn't told him about us yet. He apparently assumed that they were just having trouble and would get back together. She told him that wasn't going to happen. I think most people thought that they were meant for each other, as I did. I figured she would be back together with him when they first split up, too. Even after she fell into my arms again, I still wasn't sure. And that started up the cycle of thoughts that just wouldn't leave my head all over again.

We tried not to let anyone know at first, but living with 10 other people, I am sure the news spread a lot faster than I even knew. Finally the night came where Russ knocked on Laura's door, only to find Laura and me sitting there listening to the Dead with candles and Nag Champa burning. We weren't doing anything, but the look of guilt on both of our faces must have given us away. To his great credit, he just turned around and slammed the door behind him as he left. I felt like shit, I almost would have felt better if he had hit me. It should have been freeing. We didn't need to sneak around anymore, but my head still kept spinning.

I had to keep her. That was my only real thought. I started following her around everywhere like a lost puppy. I became very withdrawn around others or at least felt that way. My only thoughts were that I had to keep her. Of course all that accomplished was to drive her away.

I saw myself becoming all the things I never wanted to be. I became jealous of everyone and everything that competed with me for her time, like her job or her classes. I had never been a jealous, over protective boyfriend before, and I have never been one since. I hated myself for becoming that person. I could see what was happening but I couldn't stop it.

So instead of being that asshole I became completely withdrawn. I didn't speak to anyone, not even Laura. That just drove her right back to Russ. I knew it was happening and felt a helpless rage at the whole situation. The light came when I talked with my parents about my brother graduating from college. They wanted me to come back for a bit and would buy me a ticket if I knew when I wanted to go. I would leave in two weeks and planned it out so I would spend a month back in New York. When I told Laura, something very odd happened. We both just knew it would be over as soon as I left. We never said anything, we just both knew. I knew deep down it was for the best, but still didn't like it. Still, it was almost like things were much better with us those last two weeks, or maybe it was just that I had come to accept that the relationship had failed.

About three days before I left for New York, while Laura was at work, I picked up the phone and called an ex-girlfriend. She was going to be home for the summer. I already had plans with her for dinner one night.

If I Had Wings These Windmills Would Be Dead

I heard the day I left town Laura was back with Russ, but I had a great month in New York. When I came back out to Eugene I moved into a co-op right off of campus. Laura and Russ had already moved into a house on the other side of town. Russ came to the co-op all the time. We never actually talked about what had happened, but things were good between us. I didn't see Laura as much and when I did, we were always very friendly, but I still felt those pains of obsession.

Eventually I moved back to New York, and met other women. I had learned my lesson, I played things cool. For years my stomach would knot up when I thought of Laura but after a time, I gave it up to the forgiving mantra of "the stupidity of youth." I had always hoped I would run into Russ at a Dead show. Years later Laura and I got in touch. It was good to know she had some fond memories of our time together; most of my memories were of anxiety and frustration. The only good memory I had was the smell of Nag Champa. She told me that she and Russ had lost contact, but learned from a mutual friend that Russ passed away a few years earlier. I wouldn't run into him again, but I still see him dancing whenever I am at a show

Laughter

The first time I saw him he was walking through campus wearing a black lace negligee at noon. A few months later he would become my neighbor.

Geoff was a strange cat. Did I mention he was also an albino and over six feet tall before the heels? I moved into the Lorax, a co-op across the alley from his co-op, the Campbell Club. Our houses shared a lot of meals during the summer so I got to see him all the time. I always considered myself pretty liberal and accepting of others, but the first time he sat across from me while I was eating it did seem a little strange. Strange situations made Geoff giggle. Not a regular giggle at all, it was as if two or three different people were all trying to laugh out of one mouth. "teHahehe(snort)HuHUhahaha."

He didn't always dress in drag. And he had a different personality when he wasn't in drag. If he wasn't a six foot tall albino, I wouldn't have known it was the same person the first time I saw him in Jeans and a t-shirt and truckers hat. He had a southern accent and seemed very outgoing and full of bravado. When in a sorority sweater and tennis skirt he would act like a Japanese schoolgirl. In his corset and fishnet stockings, he would strut down the road like a proud diva. The clothes definitely made the man.

We once threw a cross dressing party, just to see what he would come as. He came wearing the same skirt and blouse he had been wearing earlier in the day, but seemed very happy and comfortable in a room of people dressed out of gender. It was a strange experience for me, too. When a cute girl with a mustache grabs your tits for the first time, you remember it.

One time he had a friend over who started harassing a female house mate. The police were called, and the friend argued with the police. The friend was handcuffed and being led to the car, when Geoff suddenly burst out of the door. He was wearing a black bra and panties and nothing else.

"Hey, you take your hands off of my friend!" Geoff yelled out in his deepest male southern voice.

One of the cops drew his gun, visibly shaken by this giant Victoria's Secret albino coming at him. "Sir, Ma'am, whatever the hell you are, just go back inside and put some clothes on!" He paused as Geoff stopped dead in his tracks and looked more ridiculous than ferocious. "ummm please."

And then there was the time he instantly fell in love with the beautiful hippy drug dealer. Of course her name was Seashell. The minute she walked in the door he stood straight up, walked to the furthest point in the room from her and let out a giggled. "HaheteHoGruntHaKeke"

End of Summer

I had been living out in the western wilderness for over a year but still felt as if I were a stranger in a land of nonsensical characters. I had even taken up residency in a strange castle named after a Dr. Seuss book, The Lorax Manner. Scooter was living there with me, just in town for the summer. Lenny had already gone back to New York.

At the end of the summer, the Grateful Dead were coming into town. Shows had been scheduled the year before, but had to be canceled due to Jerry's illness. Bear had come into town earlier that year, and we were flooded with some of the absolute best LSD ever seen by man. Tornado Juice.

The stadium parking lot, the university campus and the nearby state park made this a dead heads paradise, and they started filtering into town a full week before the shows. The brightly colored buses had already started to fill the lot by the end of the week. The school's football team would have to walk down Shakedown Street to get to and from two-a-day practices. I am sure the coaches warned them not to buy any food from the hippies in the parking lot, but I like to think at least one or two of them enjoyed a tasty ganja treat.

Earlier in the summer Scooter and I saw Jerry play with his solo band in Portland. It was a good daytime show in 100 degree heat. When we pulled into the lot, we parked next to a car with NY plates. "Mt. Kisco Adzam," it said on the license plate holder. Scooter and I were both excited. It had to be someone we knew. There were a few transplants, and a few friends we thought might be on tour. We put on our Richard Nixon masks and braved the afternoon heat.

Sure enough, just a little later, we saw our friend Tim, sitting on the grass, smoking a bowl alone and checking out the scene. "Tim Kravitz, How would you like to get an ex-President high?" I asked, still wearing my Richard Nixon mask. He turned and looked at me, and I could see complete horror in his eyes. He was paralyzed with fear; I could tell he truly thought Richard Nixon was asking for a hit off his pipe. "Dude, it's just me, Chuck," I said pulling off the mask.

He still had the look of horror in his eyes. "Dude, don't ever do that again, I am flipping out." I laughed and sat down and we chatted for a bit before the show began. I didn't feel too bad about flipping him out. Back in high school he had done the whole, "You're running through a forest, the trees are zooming past you, you look up, Boom! You hit a tree." Complete with a smack to the head to me.

It turned out that it was his car we had parked next to. We met up after the show at the car, he was taking off to California and then, he hoped, Hawaii. We wished him well, and it worked. Turns out he's still in Hawaii.

I had gone up to Portland and saw a Phish show right before the Dead came to town, but it was one of their rare "off nights," so I needed some good music. I made it to the lot bright and early, saw a bunch of folks I knew from town, but hadn't run into anyone from back home yet. Just before the show I ran into Laura and Russ. They were still together, but wouldn't be for very much longer. They were in a hurry to get inside. I was still looking for some Tornado Juice, having used up my reserves over the course of the summer and not planning carefully. Russ pointed out a friend of his he was sure would have some.

That guy had some. Liquid. He had a dropper full and was just going to put one or two drops on my cookie when a car door opened behind him. A trail of way too much liquid squirted up my bare arm as he got bumped. Acid is absorbed through the skin, so I panicked and wiped it off on the closet thing I could, him. We both stood there stunned for a second. I knew I had a choice. I could freak out, or I could just kick back and enjoy the ride. I decided to try enjoying the ride.

Just then I could hear the concert starting. It seemed like really spooky noise coming out of the volcano-like stadium. I did not want to go in. I handed my ticket to the first person I saw with their finger up in the air, and made my way home. If I was going to flip out, I should be in a safe place.

I made my way against the flow of everyone going into the show and made it to the bridge over the Willamette. I almost made it across campus before the Tornado Juice really hit me, causing me to stop and stare at the giant fir on campus for longer than I normally would have.

If I Had Wings These Windmills Would Be Dead

As I approached the giant brick castle that was my home my head began to swim. A few of the kids who weren't deadheads at all were outside sitting on the giant wooden swing Scooter had made. Scooter did a lot for the house in one summer. He even started a vegetable garden in the front yard. A bunch of us had helped plant and take care of it, too, but the swing was all Scooter's doing. It was a good day to sit on the swing; there were a lot of freaks walking by. I tried talking to them, but I was the freakiest freak of them all, so I made my way inside and up to my room.

The show was being broadcast on the radio, so I turned it on and got into bed. The place was an absolute mess. Clothing, CDs and everything else I owned was thrown all around. I had a black and white TV, but never really used it, and it sat in the corner on a milk crate. Someone had left an old 70's Pong game in the attic, and I had set it up one night. It just sat there collecting dust ever since.

My red plastic Graffix bong stood next to the bed beside scattered pages of horrible poetry. There were little piles of stems and seeds on some of them; I looked around until I found an actual bud. Everything was starting to swirl around me. The music sounded good and seemed to keep me grounded. After I smoked a little I was feeling really good. I wanted to go back to the show.

I reached into my pockets. I had a million things in them that I didn't need. Mostly scraps of paper. I seemed to collect scraps of paper in my pocket when I trip, though I don't ever remember putting them in my pocket. I emptied everything. All I took was my cigarettes, a bag of weed, a lighter and a pile of money, I didn't know how much. I had everything I needed; I was back off to the show.

The journey back to the stadium seemed to take forever. I got lost staring at the waterfall outside the geology department for a little while. I may have even climbed the Douglas fir, but I eventually made it back to the stadium. The band was still playing their second set. People had speakers set up everywhere, and there seemed to be just as many people in the parking lot as there were before the show.

It was still light out, but the sun was starting to go down. The trip took a hold of me and I don't remember much more of that night. I danced around a fire. I played some drums. A girl I went to high school with gave me a sandwich. Even in the dark it seemed everywhere I went I saw someone I knew. I just remember feeling very happy and very safe.

The next day I went inside for the show, or at least one of the sets, I don't know which or what they played. It was a crazy scene though. I must have been tripping pretty hard, because I was sure someone said Huey Lewis was playing with them. I was tripping hard, but it turned out Huey Lewis was there, too.

That night again was just singing and dancing and eating. Everyone there was my friend; it didn't matter if I had ever met them before. At some point I remember waking up in a tent. It was light out and I had never seen that tent before. Someone else was sleeping next to me, but I took off before they woke up.

I ended up in the park next to the stadium. There were a lot of freaks there and I was having a great time. All of a sudden, one of my housemates was riding his bike by me.

"Chuck, is that you?"

"Yup."

"You haven't been home in a while."

"I've been here."

"You know you are supposed to cook dinner for the house tomorrow night, right?" We all had jobs in the house, one night a week I cooked.

"I don't cook until Thursday." Somehow I knew enough to know that.

"It's Wednesday Chuck, why don't you come back home with me?"

"Yeah, OK," I answered and we hiked off the mountain and back to the giant brick castle that was my home.

The Guru

I

"Hey man, I finally got my amp. I'm not playing out of Bob's little shit guitar amp anymore." I was psyched. The studio where I had been playing with Mugsy and Butch had a nice bass amp, but I had blown the hell out of the one Bob gave me. Mugsy and Butch had both disappeared; Mugsy out west, Butch was lost in all the local bars.

"Cool man, you should bring your bass over and you can help me learn a few tunes." Rich was an old friend I had recently run into again. He was just learning to play guitar but had real potential. I was still a novice bass player, but Rich hadn't even tried jamming with anyone yet. His sister had died a year earlier. She had a brain tumor. They said it was pretty fast from the time she first noticed the headaches until she died. It wasn't fast for Rich. He was clearly down and out of it. He was trying to throw all his frustration into his guitar. He had the makings of an excellent blues guitarist or a tragic story, or both.

"Dude, you're the bass player," the short kid with the shaved head and piercings came around from behind the coffee counter. I'm a short guy. I say I'm 5'7", but it's probably closer to 5'6". This guy was at least three inches shorter than me but he was built like a bull dog, where I was built more like a male version of Calista Flockhart. His build and style screamed tough guy, but his eyes and smile gave away his good nature. He looked like he was probably three or four years younger than me, but he probably figured we were the same age since I was still getting carded for cigarettes. Starbucks had just moved into town, and I had moved back to New York from Oregon a year earlier, so this was it as far as coffee was concerned. The kid was psyched to have the job there. It was the hot ticket in the suburbs.

Rich looked up at him and said, "Oh yeah, Chuck this is Alex, he's a drummer. We were talking about jamming, but I don't think I'm ready yet." Rich was a pretty shy and quiet guy. He was going to be a good guitarist someday, but even he knew it wasn't that day yet. Alex grabbed my hand and shook it enthusiastically, and had a huge smile on his face.

"Rich was telling me you played bass. I found a guy. A guitarist. I think he might be really really good, but I haven't heard him play yet," That seemed odd, how could he tell the guy was good when he hadn't even heard him play? It seemed like there was something he wasn't saying. He then added, "The guy wants to do a surf rock band or something. He seems really pumped up. You should talk to him." I could tell right away that Alex was a good guy. He was a guy I could jam with. He didn't seem like he was sold on the type of music, but he was sold on the guitarist.

"Surf rock, like the Beach Boys, I can't really sing." It's funny that I used to think I actually knew about music.

"No, he said it was instrumental. I don't really know. He's a bit of a strange guy. He's a little bit older; you just have to talk to him. I think he is like a genius or something. He's really really into it. He'll tell you what it's all about." Alex already had his address book out, ready to get my number. It couldn't hurt. I wasn't in a band. The last guys I played with were the Trees, an experimental band. By experimental I mean we had no idea what we were doing, and kind of learned how to play along the way.

"Sure why not, do we have a place to jam?" I reached out, took the pad and wrote my name and number. I didn't really expect much. I've talked about jamming with a bunch of people but nothing ever came of it.

"Yeah, my parents basement. PJ wants to practice in the afternoon, so it's no problem." "

Cool, sounds good to me," I said, and then a costumer walked in the door so Alex jumped back over the counter. The guy ordered a latte, and when Alex stared banging the spoon against the milk pitcher I could tell he was going to be a good drummer. When Rich and I walked out the door I turned to him and said, "Who is this Alex guy? How do you know him?" "

I just met him here the other day. He's a friendly guy and we got to talking music. I told him I knew a bass player, that's it really." Good enough review personality wise. You didn't have to love your band mates, but it helped if you liked them. I could tell I would like Alex,

If I Had Wings These Windmills Would Be Dead

if we ever got around to playing. I went home and really didn't think much about it until my phone rang that night.

"Hello."

"Hi, is Chuck there?" the voice sounded like an old man, grandfatherly almost. Deep and relaxed, with just enough scratch to give it character. Both of my grandfathers had died years before, and my father was downstairs, so I had no idea who it could be.

"This is Chuck," I more asked then said.

"Hey this is PJ. I just got off the phone with Alex from Starbucks. You maybe want to play sometime?" It sounded almost like a kid inviting another kid to the playground, but in a old wise man's voice. I could hear a beard scratching against the phone. "

Ah, sure, I'm not really all that good," I said tentatively. "I've mostly played blues and acid rock stuff; you know 10 minute versions of Fire on the Mountain, stuff like that. Alex said you wanted to form a surf band?"

"Yeah, It's not that hard. The bass is pretty straightforward. Can you stay in time?"

"Usually," I said only half kidding.

"Here, let me play you something I just came up with. It'll give you an idea." Before he even put the phone down, I could hear his amp spark to life. The reverb was obvious before he even played a note. Suddenly a piercing high pitched guitar roared to life. I could hear things that I just didn't think were possible from one guy on a single guitar. Ripping crazy chord progressions with crazier triplets thrown over them. I later learned that his old Ampeg Gemini 2 amp called it Tremolo, but to me it was reverb, and it was crazy. I was absolutely blown away. He played for about a minute and then came back on the phone. "Stuff like that. The bass line would be basically an E minor rave up."

It took me a couple of seconds to think of what to say. This guy was obviously way out of my league. There was no way I could keep up with him. "It sounds great. I'm just not sure I'm the guy you want. I'm really just starting out. I honestly don't think I could do it."

"Oh sure you can. It'll be easy. I'll teach you everything you need to know. What harm can come of it? Give it a shot and if you're not into it, you don't have to play anymore." The guy was very pumped about it. I guessed he was right. If nothing else I could find out just how much I needed to get better to play with the big boys.

"Why not? I'll give it a go. When do you want to get together?"

II

I pulled up the driveway of a nice modern home in Armonk, right off of Route 22. It had been easier to find than the crazy directions Alex had given me. Luckily at the end of his directions it said route 22, so I knew it would be easier to find it on my own. Alex was sitting on a stone wall next to his garage. He jumped up and gave me a big smile and wave. The kid sure had energy.

"Let me grab your amp for you." He popped open the back of my jeep, and effortlessly pulled out my brand new 100 pound 100 watt Fender bass amp. It had taken me all my energy to get it from my bedroom to the driveway. I grabbed my bass and followed him to a door next to the garage. He gracefully opened the door while guiding my amp into the basement. I followed, and was surprised by what I saw. The basement was long and narrow, with light blue carpeting. A ledge stuck out on one side down the entire length of the room. It was about 2 feet high, and carpeted as well. Alex put my amp on the ledge and plugged it into the power strip.

There was a beat up old drum set right next to the door. It was covered in black sharpie with the name of every band I had heard of, and many I hadn't. One crash cymbal had cracked and begun to peel downward in a spiral, like the skin of a potato.

Then there were the mannequins. Naked half women were all over the room. There were top halves, and bottom halves. Some on small stands some piled in the corner at the end. Alex saw me looking then over and quickly said, "My mom designs clothing. She had her own business for awhile. That's what all the mannequins are for."

I laughed and said jokingly, "Oh, I didn't even notice. And your modern art cymbal?"

If I Had Wings These Windmills Would Be Dead

"Oh, I got a new crash over there," he said pointing to a brand new cymbal lying on the floor. "This one gives a good sound though." He slammed a drumstick on it, and the cymbals gave a long, echoing splash. Just as I was setting up my bass, and adjusting the volume, a car came screeching up the driveway.

It was a maroon Chrysler sedan, with bluegrass music blaring out of the window. The driver was wearing a floppy green hat, with long curls of reddish brown hair wrapping their way around the brim. He wore ordinary black sun glasses, and had the long red goatee and mustache that I had spoken to on the phone. He looked a lot younger than I imagined. He was older than me, but not by too much. When he opened the door and got out, he was much taller than Alex and I. He pulled a beat up tweed guitar case out of the back seat. Alex jumped up and grabbed his amp, which didn't look too big.

"Careful with that. It's heavier than it looks," the look on Alex's face showed that it was true. He said hi to me as he rushed by to set up his guitar.

"Can I grab something?" I yelled past Alex carrying the amp inside the door.

"The duffel bag please."

I grabbed the duffel bag and headed inside. By the time I got in the door, he had a Cherry Sunburst, hollow body, Gibson 335 around his neck. He was flicking switches, and turning dials on his amp, that was also perched on the ledge. He didn't seem to notice the naked half females all around him. "Don't touch me until I figure out my polarization." It seemed like a weird thing to say, but the second he touched the strings, the amp buzzed loudly. "See, if you touch me we might get electrocuted." He flipped a switch, touched the strings, and there was just a regular zip of fingers on strings, followed by a quickly repeating echo.

He just started into a riff without saying another word. It was as if a 27 year old Dick Dale had walked into the room. Of course I didn't know who Dick Dale was until he gave me my homework assignment later that day. He ripped through three songs, beginning to end. Fingers flying in all directions. Chords echoing while a lead was being laid on top of it. It was one thing to hear it on the phone. It was another to see it live, in person. I looked at Alex, to see if he was hearing what I was hearing. He was just standing there with his mouth open. When he finished, the amp spat out a dying crackle as he turned it off. He leaned his guitar against it and said, "Let's go smoke a cigarette and talk about what we're going to do."

"The first song is going to be our theme song. We'll play it at the beginning and end of each show," PJ said without any acknowledgment that he had just blown our minds. This guy already had a theme song for us.

"I think I'm going to need more coffee, you guys want some?" PJ and I said yes, and Alex ran up the stairs to get it. PJ and I walked outside and lit up our smokes. I didn't know what to say. I knew that I would look like a fool if I tried to play with him. There was no way I could do it.

"I'll show you the bass line to the first song today. I have the other 2 on tape, take it home and see what you can come up with. Next time we play we'll work on the second tune." He was very straightforward, and didn't speak much, but that would change as we got to know each other better.

I took a long drag on my cigarette. He was being very blunt, so I would be too. "Honestly, it's going to take a lot of work. I haven't been playing bass that long. I'll try, but I don't think you'll be too happy."

He just laughed, "Good. You haven't played too long, then you're not stuck playing wrong yet. I played bass for a reggae band up in Montreal, and I've given plenty of lessons. I think I could teach you." He hadn't even heard me play yet. I was a short, skinny long haired hippy. Compared to what I just saw, I wasn't just bad, I sucked. But there was something about his absolute confidence that made me think. What if I could do it?

"OK, the first tune. E minor. A minor, then a turn around. I think I can remember the notes, but we're going to have to take it slow."

"Yeah you'll get it. The bass can be pretty simple, once you get used to it, you can throw in your own fills, for now just play what I show you."

If I Had Wings These Windmills Would Be Dead

Alex came out with the coffee, and I drank slowly, lit another cigarette. I listened to PJ tell Alex what he wanted in the first tune. There were a lot of words I didn't understand. Alex looked like he understood a third of them, but PJ was finally able to explain it so Alex got it.

When we went back inside, Alex started banging away on the drums trying to do what PJ had explained. PJ grabbed my bass and began playing. He played two notes and then bent down and adjusted all the dials on my amp. I hadn't gotten one of them right. When he started playing again, My bass sounded like it never had before. He just played single notes, nothing fancy. He would do little rolls every now and then. Over the sound of the bass and drums he shouted, "When you get more comfortable, you can throw in a bunch of fills like this." He played something that I didn't believe I would ever play.

Alex kept the beat going and PJ handed me the bass and picked up his guitar. We all started playing. I played it as simple as I could play it. Alex was very rusty, but obviously had played a lot at some point in his life. He would be playing it perfectly soon. He threw in a bunch of great fills. The whole time, PJ would be shouting out encouragement, or instructions. We played the song over and over. We, by we I mean I, were finally getting it. My fingers were burning like they never had before. I couldn't believe what I was hearing, and that I was a part of it.

When we went outside for another smoke, PJ grabbed my hands when he saw me rubbing my finger. He looked at my finger tips. Giant blisters had already formed. He laughed and took a drag on his cigarette, "You've got to start practicing a whole lot more. But here's a tip. Use a pick. All bass players for surf bands use picks. You look like someone who vowed never to use a pick, so I won't force you, but think about it."

He said it in the nicest way possible, but it pissed me off a little. I wasn't against using a pick; I just forgot to bring one. But out of sheer stubborn pride, I refused to use a pick until our first gig. It was the first time I was an idiot and didn't listen to him; unfortunately it wouldn't be the last. "Tell you what," I said finishing my cigarette. "Why don't you teach me that second song? Once we get it, we can try playing both together." I knew that I would like PJ. I knew that I would learn a lot from PJ.

Unfortunately, I knew my own nature, and I knew I would be stubborn. We would butt heads occasionally, and usually it would be because of my stupidity. I still hadn't learned the difference between Earned Authority, and Chicken Shit Authority. Looking back now I can tell you there was no Chicken Shit where PJ was concerned.

"OK. Here's the deal. We practice twice a week. You two practice at least 2 hours a day on your own. When we get a gig, we do the set list 5 times a day until the day of the gig. You got it?" No Chicken Shit at all....

III

I was talking a mile a minute all through dinner. My poor parents just nodded, and said that's nice, and truly did hope I had found something good. They had seen me excited before. I was going to go to the Air Force Academy, and be a fighter pilot when I was very young. I was going to be a geologist in high school. I was going to be a philosopher in college. Then I was going to make movies. Now, after a couple of years of fooling around, I was going to be a bass player. They hoped this might be it, but I'm sure they didn't have the highest of hopes.

After dinner I ran upstairs and played my band's two new songs over and over. I wasn't anywhere near good enough, but PJ was right, I could learn it. My fingers were burning, but I didn't go for a pick. He wouldn't win that easily. Just as I put my bass down, the phone rang. I picked it up quickly, but before I could even finish saying hello, a voice broke me off.

"OK, what is the song you least want to hear a bunch of drunks singing in a bar?" It was PJ. I thought for a half a second before the answer hit me like a ton of bricks.

"Easy. Desperado. The Eagles are OK. But drunks singing it in a bar..."

"Cool. That's exactly the tune Alex said. I'll see you on Thursday. Keep practicing." He hung up before I could ask what it was all about, but I had a feeling we were going to be playing it at our next practice.

As I pulled up Alex's driveway, I could see PJ's car was already there. I was 10 minutes early, so PJ must have been just as psyched as I was. I

If I Had Wings These Windmills Would Be Dead

could hear PJ's guitar singing Desperado as I parked. I pulled my amp out of my car, and balanced it on my knee so I could get my hands under it. Just as I got to the door, Alex came running out.

"Let me get that for you," he offered.

"I got it; if you could get my bass I would appreciate it." It's not that I wanted to carry my amp so badly, but I was balanced with its weight. If Alex grabbed it quickly from me, I was sure I'd hurt my back. PJ stood next to his Classic Ampeg Gemini II amp, with his beautiful guitar around his neck. He had a big smile as he welcomed me. I put down the bass, and PJ handed me a coffee. Alex had prepared for us this time. "So I guess we're going to play Desperado now. Show it to me over a cigarette."

PJ unplugged his guitar, but kept it around his neck as he followed me outside. Alex followed with his cup of coffee. "OK Chuck, Alex's got the drums down. Now I'll teach you the bass line. I'll be playing Desperado on guitar," he quickly played a vocal line on his unplugged guitar. "While you play the bass line to the Chicago tune 25 or 6 to 4." He played the bass line on his guitar, and I knew exactly what he was talking about. It was a fairly simple bass line, one I knew I could play, and it would sound great with the guitar. I put my cigarette out after only a few drags, and went inside and began fiddling with it. There were some changes in the song, but once I got them the song would be great. A surf rock version of Desperado.

Alex came in and joined us on drums. His beat was perfect. Straightforward, with just enough ride on the cymbals. PJ finished his cigarette, then came and joined in. By the fifth or sixth time through, I really got the idea. PJ then switched gears and we learned the third song he had written. At one point, one of us referred to Alex as Skooby. Pretty soon we made a joke about him getting us more coffee for Twooo Skooby Snacks. PJ jumped up immediately. "We are the Skooby Snacks. That's perfect; all my bands have been named after food."

I knew his most recent band had been Pork Chop. From PJ's description they sounded like a Bluegrass/Jug music band. PJ would call out names of players I had never heard of who were influences. Dock Boggs, Flatt and Scruggs, Gus Cannon, and the list went on. I tried to make a note of all the names for future reference. I thought over Skooby Snacks. It sounded good to me, but Alex shot down the idea immediately.

"People might think it's a reference to cocaine. Maybe we should come up with something else, considering I'm in AA," It was his first mention of that. It seemed like he was trying to find the perfect time to say something. I wasn't sure what to say, but PJ broke the silence.

"OK, let's scrap the Skooby Snacks. I hope you don't mind that I drink. Cause I love to drink. What about you Chuck?" Both of them looked at me like I was the final vote on if we all drink or not.

"Well, I like to have a few beers, but I've always been more of a pot smoker. I hope you guys don't mind."

"Yeah, like I couldn't tell that by how many times I had to show you the same changes," PJ said quickly with a laugh. "I don't mind. I smoke on a very rare occasion. My wife likes to smoke, she smokes, and I drink, and I don't take her weed, and she doesn't drink my beer. It's a perfect relationship." Now we both looked at Alex to see what his reaction would be.

"Oh I don't care what you guys do. All my friends drink and smoke. The only reason I gave up pot was they don't let you do that in AA. But you guys drinking or smoking won't pressure me into it. I only really went to AA when I first quit, they helped then, but now I don't really need the help."

We went outside to smoke our final cigarette and talk about the day's progress. We kept talking about our different vices, and how ridiculous we have been to supply them in the past. I mentioned smoking pot out of a coke can with holes poked in it while working at a country club.

Alex laughed hard. "I was working in a gas station, and we had a pipe, but no screen. One of the guys working there said 'wait, we have a whole roll of screening in the back,' He took a pair of scissors and went into the garage. He came out with the perfect circular screen for the pipe." Alex was cracking himself up as he told the story. "So we smoked, and we got wasted. Way higher than we should have smoking pot. Then we all got headaches. Then we all got sick. We found out later that the screen was used to filter anti-freeze, and that's what got us so fucked up." By the end of his story we were all cracking up. PJ actually looked like a light bulb went off in his head.

"Well then, I guess we're just going to have to name the band after the antifreeze, "The Presstones."

Phish Tour

We practiced at least two times a week for the next few weeks. Each time, we would learn 2 new songs, and play all the songs we had learned to that point. PJ had written a couple of Latin American inspired songs, and we worked on some surf standards. Alex was catching on very fast. He was a talented drummer, and he was getting better and better. Slowly his crash cymbal was unraveling; the crack had already made two laps around the circumference of the outer edge.

I wasn't very happy with my progress, but PJ was encouraging. I kept forgetting changes in our old songs, and not remembering new songs the next practice. Physically my fingers were getting better. I could add rolls, and even played a couple of solos. The first was a solo PJ wrote. It was an original surf tune we called Skip the 30's. PJ already had a plan in his head, this song would be early in the show and both Alex and I would get a little solo. I was having real trouble coming up with something and I'm sure PJ had something in mind all along, so he just jumped in and showed me what to play. Of course it was perfect.

"Play this, "he ran up a few slow scales, and it was simple and beautiful. "Do you think you can play that?"

"Not note for note, but I can jam off those scales." We went through the song again, and while I never played exactly what he had shown me, it was a great little riff. The other solo was in a fast version of Bob Dylan's Lay Lady Lay. That was a simple progression, so I played a little something different every time. I kind of expected PJ to get pissed at that, but he didn't. Our practice sessions were the closest I had come to school since Oregon, and PJ played up the part as favorite teacher. Alex and I learned as much from him sitting outside smoking cigarettes as we did actually playing music. He wasn't into just bluegrass; he was into every type of music ever played.

I was not a neophyte when it came to music. I had worked in record stores before, and I'm the type of person who picks up something from everyone. I was a big Phish and Grateful Dead fan, and because they both played so many types of music and I tried to learn as much as I could about all of them, I thought that I knew a thing or two about music. I'm sure I did tell PJ something about music he didn't know, but it was as if I gave him a penny, and he gave me 100 bucks. It was not a very even exchange. PJ had heard of Phish, but wasn't really impressed. Unfortunately he would dislike Phish even more, when they started taking time out of our practice sessions.

The spring Phish tour was coming. At that point, most of the money I would make throughout the year would come from the parking lot of Phish or Dead tours, so I saw going on tour as a must. PJ saw it as a couple of weeks that we wouldn't be practicing. Plus I was finally getting the songs we had learned down. After two weeks he was afraid I would forget everything I learned. When I told both he and Alex that I would be gone, they decided to still get together once or twice to come up with new songs. That was fine by me; I thought at least it wouldn't be time wasted, but they both thought differently.

I was going to be traveling in a car with Lenny, Rich and some former Marine I had never met, and we had decided that we would work together to make the most money possible. We worked out a four-pronged attack, none of which was entirely legal. The first, and closest to an actual legal plan was the shirts. Lenny and I bought 300 white t-shirts at a great price, then immediately called our buddy Chris in Rochester. He was a student at RIT and one hell of an artist. He had all the tools he needed at school, and told us he already had a design. All we would need to do is get to Rochester with the shirts, and silkscreen three hundred times. We would give Chris a percentage, but we could basically sell the shirts that originally cost pennies, for 20 bucks each.

The second idea was the grilled cheese sandwiches. Everyone sold food in the parking lot before the show. The problem was everyone sold out early, and after the show there was no food to be found. We wouldn't sell a single sandwich before the show, but right as the second set was coming to a close, we would run out and get the hibachi fired up. At two bucks each, we couldn't make them fast enough as all the Phish heads came out of the venue. The bread was free, thanks to a very trusting delivery guy at the local supermarket. He would drop

If I Had Wings These Windmills Would Be Dead

bags of bread in front of the store at three thirty in the morning. The first employee didn't show until five. So we had a nice hour and a half window. The best part was, if we were in the bar down the street, the bread man would stop there first, and then we could just follow him to the market. I think whenever the Dead or Phish were in the city; the entire town of Bedford would be without bagels. I know we weren't the only ones to do that. Eventually the bread man was given a key, so he could leave the bread in the store. All good things come to an end.

The third idea was the beer. Go to the beer distributor in whatever town you happen to be in. Look for the best deal on good beer. You can usually find Brooklyn beer, or Sierra Nevada, or something good on special. Now all you need is a skateboard, a cooler, and a few bags of ice and you are a portable beer man. If you can get a couple of cases of good beer for 15 bucks each, and then sell them at 3 bucks a pop, you're going to have a good night.

I had been on a few Phish tours, and a few Dead tours. You get to know a lot of people on tour, especially if you've got beer and T-shirts. The forth way of making money, though the most illegal, is the easiest. Find the guy on tour with the most pot. Work out a deal so that you get something for everyone you send his or her way. I knew one girl who had the best thing going on tour. We worked out a great deal, and sure enough, at least once a show, I'd run into a friend who had a lot of money, but hadn't found anything good yet. I'd send them her way, and at the end of the night she'd give me either cash, or bud, or both, depending on what I needed the most. I was never worried about getting busted or anything, since I never actually sold a thing, and everyone I sent to her I already knew from home or school, or tour.

Canadian Mule

Rich was supposed to warn us before we got to the border. Lenny and I each had a half a gram of pot wrapped in tin foil and we wanted to finish it before coming back into the US. Lenny Rich and I all knew each other from high school. Gabe was pretty much a complete stranger. He was in the Marines, from Colorado, and, we would learn after a week on the road together, a homophobic racist.

We were coming back from a Phish show in Montreal. We were going to be selling T-shirts all week to pay for the trip and the first leg went well. We didn't bring any pot into Canada, and didn't want to leave with any either. Lenny and I each bought the smallest amount we could on the parking lot, and then smoked as much as we could before a long late night car ride back to the states.

Rich woke us up right as we were pulling into the border checkpoint. Lenny and I shot each other nervous glances, but there would only be trouble if we were searched and what were the odds of that. Hopefully Rich would say all the right things...

"What was the reason for your visit to Canada?" asked the man in the uniform.

"We were at a Phish show," replied Rich, the one answer sure to get us searched. First they searched the car and found the Phish shirts. It took a while, but we convinced them that they were made in the USA and they dropped it. I kept waiting for a moment where I could ditch the weed but they were watching us like hawks. I thought they might let us go after searching the car, but no, we were ordered inside with two of the border agents.

One told the rest of us to sit while the other took Lenny in back to be searched first. Gabe immediately started talking about local hunting spots with the remaining agent and distracted him long enough for me to pull the small foil pouch out of my pocket and shove it into the grill of the radiator behind me.

Just then the first agent came back with Lenny in cuffs. The three of us and the other agent all turned to look as the first agent showed us the smallest bag of marijuana ever confiscated by police. Just then I heard what seemed to be an extremely loud "plink." The small pouch of pot that I placed in the radiator must have expanded when the heat turned on and fired out of the grill, flew over my shoulder and landed in the middle of the floor.

Neither agent saw it. Rich was closest to it. He stretched his leg out and calmly covered it with his foot, then slowly drew it back towards him. Suddenly the first agent turned to me and pointed. My heart stopped; sure he had caught something out of the corner of his eye. "Get up and come with me." I followed him into a small room where he made me strip and bend over. He shined a flashlight up my ass. "OK. Get dressed." We went back and he called Rich in next. As Rich stood up I expected to see the tin foil come out from under his foot but it was gone.

After paying all of our t-shirt money to get Lenny free, we were on our way, but I like to think there is still a tin foil pouch of weed somewhere inside that border checkpoint.

Harmful or Fatal if Swallowed

Despite the financial setback, seeing Phish play completely different shows every night always blew my mind. I would dream of being in a band that doesn't have to play the same songs every night. I was taking notes at every show. Seeing how they played with the crowd. How Trey would give the fans signals on guitar and the fans would react. I thought that somehow we could use this. I couldn't wait to get back with the band.

I told PJ all about it when I got back. Again I was all excited, talking up a storm, but PJ didn't seem that excited. He tried to explain that he liked doing quick songs, in and out. Surf music was a different animal. He was very familiar with the Dead, so he knew what I was trying to say, but he was rejecting it as nicely as he could. He had a very firm idea of what the Presstones should be. Being young and stupid, I thought I knew better about what people would want to hear. It was obvious we had two different ideas about live shows.

The next practice, PJ came in with a new song. He ripped a great version of Superstition on his guitar. It was short, but it sounded great. He showed me what he thought the bass line should be. The second I heard it, I could only think of Flashlight by Parliament. I changed it a bit, to make it even closer to the Parliament tune, and it rocked, from the first time we played it together. The break for Phish tour actually helped me. By not playing bass, I had thought of nothing but playing bass. I didn't even realize at the time that Superstition was just PJ throwing me a bone. If I wanted to get a little funky, fine, but only on that tune.

"Hey Alex, did you take this picture," PJ was looking through a manila folder that Alex had thrown on the carpeted ledge. For the first time Alex was the last one to practice, luckily his brother was there to let in PJ and me. We had a nice ten minute long jam to warm up before Alex finally got home. He was taking classes at SUNY Purchase while working at Starbucks. One of his classes was photography, and I could see

"Yeah, I took all of those at school the other day. Is that the two chicks?" Alex asked while getting behind his drums without even looking at what PJ was holding. He held the picture for me to see, and sure enough it was two girls. They were each bundled in winter clothes, wearing hats and scarves. It was the beginning of spring, but that winter continued to fight for survival. Both girls had round faces, with their eyes closed. They both had their tongues sticking out, and they were just barely touching. PJ held the photo with his fingers framing just the faces.

"That would make a pretty good album cover wouldn't it," PJ looked at up at us and Alex got excited. He jumped out from behind the drums and grabbed the picture.

"I thought the same thing. There is something about those two girls. It's not sexy, but it kind of is. They are kind of cherubic, don't you think? I can get my girlfriend to work it up on her computer. She's good at that stuff." PJ and I just glanced at each other with a chuckle. We had met her once. PJ was happily married, and I have always tried to be politically correct, or at least not a pig, but there was only one word we could use to describe her. Tits. She was a very attractive girl, slim waist long black hair, and she was very nice, but the only thing we could remember about her was her tits. They were too large. They must have caused back pain. For PJ and me to have talked about it, and had a bit of a laugh over it, they had to be large. On the day we met her, she was wearing a shirt that did not hide them at all, either. Alex's voice snapped us both back. "What do you think? Do we have enough songs to try recording them? Are we ready for a studio?"

"Let me call my buddy Dale. We could record a tape right here on a four track. He's a genius with recording. The first day he's available we can do it. If you guys could handle recording 15 tunes in a day. We can't waste Dale's time." He looked up to see our reaction. When neither of us said anything, he added "Now you two warm up while I go take a crap." PJ put the photo down and went up the steps. Alex started up a beat, and I just started playing a little funky riff to it. Soon it morphed into a kind of sideshow type of thing. From the top of the stairs we could hear PJ yelling, "Keep going I'm thinking of something for that."

If I Had Wings These Windmills Would Be Dead

Alex and I kept going, and PJ finally joined us. He jumped right in with a great jazz guitar riff, and we had a tune written within minutes. We kept playing it, until it had a beginning, middle and end. The song had a carnival barker, or snake oil salesman feel to it, so we called it Limited Time Offer. Once we had it down we did every tune we had ever played together in one stretch. PJ was ready before we had our first practice, but Alex and I were finally ready, too.

When the day came to record, Rich came with me. He had been playing a lot of guitar, but felt like he wasn't getting anywhere. I knew that just by meeting PJ he'd be a better guitarist. To me, he sounded like he had gotten better, but I knew how it was. The fingers got better, but you felt as if there was something more just out of your grasp.

A couple of weeks earlier, Rich had signed a lease with Lenny and two other guys on a house in Pound Ridge. It was in the middle of the woods and miles from anything. Within three days he had moved out. He claimed his girlfriend Rebecca didn't like the place, and that he had allergies. Really I think he felt bad about leaving his mother and sister so soon after his other sister had died. Rebecca lived close to Rich's mom in Mount Kisco, almost a half hour away from the house in Pound Ridge, so at the time I thought she may have had something to do with it, but I would find out later that she didn't.

PJ arrived with Dale. Dale looked like an old prospector, with long curly hair, and a long curly beard. He had an old rumpled leather hat with a wide brim that hid his eyes. PJ introduced him, but he walked right inside and began setting up mics. I went to see if I could help and PJ stopped me. "He knows what he's doing. You'll just get in the way." It must have looked like I took offense to what he said so he quickly added, "I'd get in the way, too."

When we walked inside Dale had both PJ and my amps wired up, and he was working on the drums. He only had one mic stand, and was cursing himself under his breath until he noticed all of the naked half mannequin's lying on the ground. In no time at all he had a microphone duct tapped to the crotch of one facing the bass drum, and had other mics tapped to hands and feet pointing at other drums. He had us play one song, while listening carefully in his headphones and adjusting knobs. Finally he spoke his first words to us. "All set when you are."

We began with the Presstone's Theme and ripped through 6 straight songs. I was pumped up and felt like I had done a good job. There were a few minor screw-ups, but PJ told me to worry about it at the end. Rich was absolutely blown away. Only Alex's family and girlfriend had heard us play, so I was waiting to show off my new band to someone.

When we went out to smoke a cigarette, Dale and PJ just started swapping stories. It turned out Dale played mandolin in PJ's old Jug band. By the time the day was done we had 13 songs recorded. To this day I can still hear my worst error, but for the most part it couldn't have gone better. Alex played his ass off, I got everything down as well as I possibly could, Rich got a new guitar teacher, and PJ got an extra 20 bucks a week.

It worked out that if each of us paid Dale 100 bucks, he would make us 200 tapes. It seemed fair enough. The tapes would only cost about a hundred bucks, but Dale was putting a lot of work into it. It would take him a week or so to even mix all the instruments right. Alex's girlfriend could start making the inserts and we would be all set.

"Great day everyone. Oh, yeah guys, I got us a gig." I had been holding it back all day. "My brother is getting his masters, and my parents want to have a party at their house. They'll pay us to play, and we can sell some tapes. So we need to get two sets worth of songs and we have one month to get ready."

The Ballad of Rich and Rebecca

The first time I was on TV was at Rich's 8th birthday party. His parents took us to Yankee Stadium, and Dave Winfield stole a homerun from a batter by leaping and catching the ball right as it was headed for my face. It became a highlight clip for the Yankees of the 80's. Thirteen years later, Rich was down and out.

He was still dealing with his sister's death. He kept trying to move on, but he wasn't ready. His surviving sister had turned her depression into physical illness. She was being treated for Lyme disease, but the doctors could not find anything wrong with her. Rich was turning to drinking and pot smoking, and he did both as if they were going out of style. The only problem was that he turned into a zombie when he smoked. If he was driving, you could tell him to turn left, and he just kept going straight. The only really good thing he had going for him was Rebecca.

Rebecca was the younger sister of a classmate of ours. She was only eighteen and a senior in high school, but she had a much older soul. Her father had died when she was very young, and her mother took very little interest in her daughter's life. It made her grow up a little too fast. She wasn't considered a beauty queen, but she was definitely cute. Her sweet disposition and infectious smile made her beautiful once you got to know her. Most of our friends would have gotten a lot of shit from us for dating a high school girl, but Rebecca was such a sweetheart that no one even mentioned it too much. She didn't drink or smoke, but that made her seem more mature. Other friends of mine were dating younger girls, but she just didn't seem like a younger girl.

Rich was taking her for granted. We could all see it. He was her first love, and it seemed as if she'd do anything for him. He was working detailing cars, and would go to the bars almost every weeknight. Rebecca had school the next day, so she would never be out with him. Even though they did spend time together, I never really saw them together. I only saw them together a few times, but I ran into her almost everywhere I went.

One night, while sitting at the diner with Lenny, she walked in with one of her friends that neither of us had met. We called them over and they sat down with us. Lenny is a bit of a dog when it comes to women, and I could tell right away that he was interested in Rebecca's friend. She was fairly tall, blonde and dressed in almost a business suit. He barely said anything to her that night, but the next day he was on the phone with Rich trying to find out about her.

Her name was Tina, and she was going to take over the world one day. She had already been accepted at Lehigh, and was going to be an international business lawyer. She was the complete opposite of Lenny, who was a deadhead, and major pot smoker. Somehow they ended up together. It really was a case of opposites attract. For the next few weeks, Rich, Rebecca, Tina and Lenny were out with each other every day. Unfortunately Rich wasn't too happy. He had met a couple girls at the bar, and secretly told me that he wanted to end it with Rebecca. I told him it was a mistake, but the next day he ended it anyway.

According to Lenny and Tina she was heartbroken. It had taken her totally by surprise. Rich hadn't been too nice about it either. He told Rebecca that she was boring, and he wanted to see other girls. Within a week, Rich had realized his mistake. The girls at the bar were not as into him as he thought. I didn't know it at the time, but he began calling Rebecca trying to get back together.

Rebecca was pissed. She had completely trusted Rich, and never expected him to treat her so badly. Meanwhile, Tina and Lenny were doing everything that they could to cheer her up. Rebecca's birthday was coming up, and she had gotten 4 tickets to go see Melissa Etheridge. Because she did not ever want to see Rich again, Lenny and Tina asked me if I wanted to go. I didn't think anything would come of it, or I probably wouldn't have gone. The night was pretty uneventful. The concert was good, but nothing special. At the end of the night, as we dropped Rebecca off at home, she turned to me and gave me a quick peck on the check. It was more sisterly than anything. I wished her a happy birthday and she ran off inside.

A couple of days later my phone rang, and it was Rebecca. She was coming to the end of her senior year, and the prom was coming up. She nervously told me how she already bought a dress expecting to go with Rich. She was not the most social girl in the world, and she told me that she had not found anyone else to go with.

If I Had Wings These Windmills Would Be Dead

"I had a great time at the concert. I was just wondering if maybe you would go to the prom with me." I was 22 years old at the time, and I had only gone to my own prom for about 20 minutes. I was thinking about what to say when she added, "I already got the tickets, and Tina and I were planning a trip to Block Island the next day. All you would need to do is rent a tuxedo. Lenny is going to, so you wouldn't even need to talk to anyone else. We only have to be there for a short time."

Without even thinking of the consequences, I agreed and then called Lenny. He was excited about it. He and Tina still had not slept together, and he was sure that prom night would be the night. The prom was not the only thing he wanted to talk about.

"My roommate Jack is moving out. He had a fight with my other roommate, and he just left. Pete and I can't afford the rent by ourselves. Do you want to move in?" I had a bunch of money burning a hole in my pocket from the Phish tour, so I agreed. In one hour, without even thinking about it, I had "stolen Rich's Girl" and moved into the house that he had rented, then moved out of. Although I was happy to have so much going on, it would not go down in history as my proudest day.

The House on the Ridge

The house was a monument to horrible mid-sixties architecture, built with entire walls of glass. It sat on top of a big hill in the middle of the woods. It was secluded, even though it was right off High Ridge Road, a pretty major route from Pound Ridge to Stamford. The driveway also serviced a big beautiful white colonial house, with a large green lawn right off the road. As you passed that house the driveway continued up a hill, and seemingly into the trees. As you entered the woods there was a small, dark wooden cottage right off the driveway. Landlord Mike the lawyer lived there. Mike was a strange guy. He wouldn't leave the house for two weeks, and then he'd be gone for three days at a time. He had a girlfriend, who would stand just outside the door smoking a cigarette, and looking a little too much like a prostitute in the middle of the woods.

The driveway made a sharp turn past the cottage, went up an even steeper slope, and then snaked between two large trees. The drive led to a large flat paved area lined with birch trees at the top of the hill. There was a small pile of wood with an axe stuck in a large stump on the far side of the parking area. The house looked like a long red wooden wall, broken up into three parts. The parts arched along the parking area like an outfield wall.

The small first part was one story, and only looked about 10 feet long. Stone and cement separated it from the next part, which was at least two stories high, and was by far the longest section of the house. There were two tall narrow windows in this part. The only windows visible. The third section did not even look one story high, but it was very long, almost as long as the middle section. The only door was on the third section, right where it met the second.

The door swung in, blocking your view of the large section as you entered. Looking to the left you would see a long dark hallway, with three doors on the right, and a door at the end. The floor was stone chips embedded in concrete. The paint was very dark, and the sight did not inspire a very welcoming feeling. Closing the door revealed one of the oddest living areas I have ever seen.

If you walked along the right, there was a fairly wide walkway made of stone, leading to the first section of the house, which was hidden by a large stone wall. That, except for the extremely high ceiling, was not too far out of the ordinary. It was what was to your left that was amazing. There were two sets of stairs. The first went up to a loft that was as wide as the entire section. There were iron railings along the entire stretch. You could not see how far the loft went back, but you could tell that the sun was shining through the far end.

There were three steps leading down to a sunken area. The far end was covered in bookshelves, with a fireplace in the middle. The loft hung over two thirds of the pit, but it was high enough not to make the pit feel too claustrophobic. There was a sofa, and a TV, and then the most unexpected thing. Between the "pit" and the walkway was a huge iron box, with a large pipe going all the way up through the ceiling. It was the largest wood-burning stove I had ever seen. This was the heat for the entire house. The stove would heat pipes in the floor, which radiated through all three sections of the house.

The loft ended up being a lot bigger than I expected. In the middle of the loft, directly above the fireplace in the pit, was a fireplace with an open back, so that people in the front and the back of the loft could enjoy the fire. There was a dining room table in the first half, overlooking the rest of the house; the second half had two sofas looking out over the back end of the loft, which was an entire glass wall. The ceilings were noticeably black with soot, presumably from the stove. There must have been a leak somewhere in that chimney.

This was going to be Rich's room when they were originally going to have four people move in. It didn't give much privacy, which might have been one of the things bugging him about the place. The view was beautiful from the glass wall. It overlooked a heavily forested valley.

The kitchen was housed in the first section, and was also bigger than you would have thought from outside. It had semi-modern white cabinets, and all new appliances. One wall was glass, with a door leading to a stone patio. The patio looked out over part of the driveway, but was unnoticeable as you were driving up.

If I Had Wings These Windmills Would Be Dead

The third section of the house held the bedrooms. If all the doors were closed, there was no light in the hallway, but when you opened the doors, The hallway was bathed in sunlight as they all had walls of windows. The second bedroom would be mine, and looking out the window made me feel as if I had just opened a tent, and was in the middle of a forest floor. There was a small bathroom, with a shower. The room at the end of the hall was the master bedroom. It had a huge bathroom, a fireplace, and 2 walls of glass. That was Pete's room. He was going to pay more to have that room, but it was worth it. The loft and the master bedroom both had the feeling of being above the forest, while the other two rooms felt like they were in the forest.

The house was odd enough, but then there was Pete...

The Naked Chick

Lenny and I had been driving looking for wood all night. It was cold as hell with a couple of inches of snow on the ground, but it was warmer in my truck than it was in the house. We had run out of wood again.

"There's some." Lenny pointed to a haphazardly thrown together pile of logs. We could see construction vehicles down the wooded dirt driveway. There was a lot of new construction going on. They probably cleared the lot before construction. We got out, threw as much of it as would fit in the back of the Jeep Cherokee and headed back to the house.

We quickly got the fire going again, but it would take a little while to warm up the house. We decided to get back into the warm car and take the ten minute drive to the diner in Stamford. Most of the drive was down dark, winding, sparsely populated roads. There were no other cars at that time of night. Suddenly, out of the corner of my eye, I thought I saw a naked girl in the bushes on the other side of the road.

"Did you see that?" I asked Lenny.

"See what?"

"A naked chick?"

"Dude, you're crazy. There was no naked chick." Lenny seemed pretty sure, but I turned the car around anyway. "There's no naked chick on the side of the r..." He trailed off as we rounded a curve and there in the middle of the road was a naked chick. Well, she wasn't completely naked. She was wearing a red silk nightie, but barefoot on the icy road. As I pulled over and started rolling down the window to ask her if she needed help, she ran over and opened up the back door and got in without a word.

We were pointed back towards the house, and I just started driving. "Umm, Hi. Can we bring you somewhere?"

"Heat," she finally shouted as she jumped in between the front seats to hold her hands in front of the vents on the dashboard. "Where were you guys going?"

"We were going to the diner, but we are turned around now going back towards our place."

"Do you have heat at your place? Can we go there for a bit? I can go back home after he cools down." She told us a long story about how she was a model (I had only glimpsed her before she got in the car and it was too dark to see in the car, but she very well could have been.) She was a former marine. She had a Husky that had been stolen and she was tracking it down to a dog fighting ring in Connecticut somewhere. Her roommate had done a lot of drugs and thought she should sleep with him for cheaper rent so she ran outside in the freezing cold half naked. She had no idea how long she had been out there.

When we got back, the whole house hadn't been heated yet, but the stove was firing out heat and the area around it was getting hot. She ran right to the stove. "Careful that gets hot," but before we could finish, she wrapped herself around the metal chimney pipe coming out of the top. We thought she would scream in pain, but instead she rubbed her silken nightie-clad model body all over it like she was doing a pole dance.

"I smell weed, can I smoke weed?" Sure, why not? We smoked some weed with her. "I have some coke, do you want some coke?" She was almost naked, where did she have coke, yet from somewhere she suddenly had a folded up paper in her hand. Coke wasn't my thing, and I don't think Lenny had ever done it before, so we both declined but told her to feel free. She broke up a couple of lines on a CD cover, and then quickly snorted it all. As she looked up she noticed Lenny's weight bench in the corner. She shot straight up, lay on the bench, unpantied beaver pointed right at us and started bench pressing.

When she stopped lifting she came back over to the table and talked for an hour straight. It all sounded like more and more bullshit. The girl was bat shit insane and I think it was way more than just the drugs doing it to her. Finally she noticed the exchange of "how the fuck do we get rid of her" glances Lenny and I were giving each other. She mentioned that her roommate might be asleep by now. I grabbed my keys and we headed out.

If I Had Wings These Windmills Would Be Dead

We dropped her off at a house that was at least a fifteen minute walk from where we picked her up. It was no wonder why she pole-danced the chimney.

Ballad of Rich and Rebecca Part II

"Hey PJ, is your wife coming to the gig?" Alex had a smile on his face. We had not met PJ's wife, and we we're beginning to make jokes that he only wore a wedding ring to meet women. "Or is she grading papers?" She was a teacher at an all girls' high school in Greenwich.

"No, she'll be there, but my first wife ran off with my bass player. If I see you even look at her you're dead," he said looking right at me. Alex laughed thinking it was a joke. I had told them about Rebecca, but hadn't been able to tell Rich yet. Rich's birthday was the day before. I went over and had cake with him; got him a cool guitar care kit and felt guilty every second I was there. I was looking for the perfect time to tell him. PJ had yelled at me, telling me I had already waited too long. We thought he was just talking about that when he said, "I'm serious. She was a crazy Portuguese chick I met after college. We we're living in Montreal and I was playing in a blues band, when one day I came home. She told me she was leaving me, and poof, she was gone. The worst part was we played a couple of more gigs together. I couldn't even look at him.

I had pissed PJ off. In the past we had played games where we tried to piss each other off a little bit, but this was different. Alex knew about Rebecca, but really didn't say much except, "Dude, is she cute?" He wasn't really thinking when he pushed PJ further to tell more. Luckily he was more curious about PJ's current wife.

"Well I left Montreal shortly after that. Lucy was a friend of mine up at Cornell, like a best friend. I was living in Long Island, and she moved up from Maryland. We stayed friends for a long time, and then one day we just decided to hook up. We've been married 2 and half years. We moved up here when she got a job in Greenwich. I was lucky to get my job at WARC." He worked as a music teacher for a school for adults with mental disabilities. I often joked that was the only reason he could be so patient with me. "OK, now we have to get Pomp and Circumstance down for your brother. He is going to make a speech or toast or something right."

"If I know my brother, he'll be making speeches and toasts all day and night." The party was three days away. We had 30 short as hell songs. It would go quick, but it would be just about perfect for an afternoon party. "Hey PJ, didn't you have some western ballad thing you were working on. Let's give that a try, that will help lengthen the show."

PJ more or less laid down an ultimatum. He had a lesson with Rich the next day, and if I didn't tell Rich about Rebecca, he would. I really couldn't let that happen. I had been hanging out more and more with Rebecca, and I was starting to really like her. At first I was thinking that we would just go to the prom and nothing would happen, so it wouldn't be a big deal. I was doing it as a favor to Lenny and Tina as much as for Rebecca. But it was becoming obvious that the prom would not be the end of things for us. I was kind of hoping I wouldn't have to tell Rich until after my brother's party. He had been to a few practices and our recording session, and he was pumped to see us play in front of a crowd.

I tried to tell PJ that, but he just kept saying the sooner I told Rich the better. That night I called him, and he immediately asked to come over. He always sounded a little down, but he didn't sound pissed. Part of me was hoping he already knew, but he didn't. He wasn't pissed when I told him I was moving into the house, and I didn't expect him to be. It was Rebecca that would probably piss him off. I had no idea how he would react. I told him to come on over. I had already picked up some beers. Rebecca had told me earlier that she might come over, so I called her and told her not to come. I was going to tell Rich. She breathed a sigh of relief. She was just as nervous about telling him as I was. A few days earlier she had offered to tell him, but I could see in her eyes that she really didn't want to.

Pete was working, and Lenny was at Tina's house, so I had the place all to myself. Almost an hour later Rich pulled into the driveway. When he came in he looked tired, but not mad. He didn't know. "Man it was a tough day at work today. Then I get home and my mom is bitching about everything. I just had to get out of the house." He wasn't making it easy for me. I told him to sit down; I gave him a packed pipe and went into the kitchen to get him a beer.

If I Had Wings These Windmills Would Be Dead

The whole time he was talking about all the assholes at work. It was as worked up as I'd ever heard him. Once he smoked a little he would calm down, but I was pretty sure that I'd end up getting a fist in my face before the end of the night. I was OK with that. There have been a couple of times in my life when I deserved to get hit, and this was one of them.

By the time I got back to the "pit" Rich looked a little more relaxed. A string of smoke was rising up from the pipe, which was now sitting on the coffee table. I handed Rich his beer and took a long drink from mine. I had drunk two beers while waiting for him, and now I was killing my third. I took a big hit on the pipe and built up a combination of "Irish and Dutch" courage. "Rich, there's something I got to tell you."

"What's that," he coughed between inhaling and exhaling the smoke.

"Well, you know how I went with Lenny, Tina, and Rebecca to the Melissa Etheridge show."

"Yeah."

"Well, a week or so later Rebecca called me and asked me to go to the prom. I said yes. Nothing's happened between us, but I wanted to tell you. She told me she had no one else to go with, and I figured Lenny would rather I go than hang out with a bunch of high school kids all night." I was probably speaking too fast. I looked up at Rich, and his eyes were wide open.

"Tell her you can't go." His voice was rising, and he started to get up. "I can't do that. I already said yes. She's got her dress and the tickets and everything. The prom is in two weeks. I can't back out now." His eyes went from wide open to clenched squinting. He stood up fast, and slammed his beer down on the table. It spilled all over. I stood up, and tried to calm him down, but he just turned and walked to the door.

"Well then fuck you," he said as he left. I tried to get him to come back, but he just got in his car and sped down the driveway.

I immediately thought of Rebecca. I was hoping he wouldn't go over there, but he might. I called her, to see if anyone else was at her house just in case. She had four sisters, including a twin, and an older brother, so I was sure she wasn't alone, but I wanted to make sure. One of her older sisters was dating a friend of Rich's and they were both there. I figured since he didn't hit me, he probably would not even threaten her at all, but I still felt better. If Rich's buddy was there too, he would help keep the peace if Rich did show up.

Two hours later my phone rang and it was PJ. Rich had gone to his house when he left mine. PJ said that he was really pissed, but PJ calmed him down a little. I knew that PJ could, he was always a voice of reason with the soothing tone to his voice. Rich had told him that he had been calling Rebecca every night since they broke up trying to get back with her. This took me by surprise. Around me I guess he was trying to be the tough guy saying that he liked being free, and now he could hook up with anyone he wanted. I knew that part of that was a front, but Rebecca never told me that he was still calling.

I had almost finished a twelve pack of beer, and smoked way too much since Rich had left, and PJ could tell. "Hey don't worry about it. It may take him awhile, but he won't be pissed at you forever." That was a different tone than he was using at practice. I guess now that I had told Rich, it was at least a little better in his eyes. "I'll talk to him some more, try to smooth things out. Just let him be pissed for a while. There's not a lot you can do, so you should get a good night's sleep, and then come to practice ready to play tomorrow."

For a couple of weeks I didn't see Rich at all. Some mutual friends would approach me saying that Rich was pissed at me and called me an asshole. I never argued. Yes, I knew I was an asshole. When I walked into a bar one night weeks later, Rich was sitting at the far end. He never said a word to me, and left as soon as he finished his beer. It was going to take a long time. I wished he had hit me, and gotten it over with all at once.

Kentucky Fried Pete

It is very safe to say that Pete was a little weird. A little is putting it very lightly. Pete had a pet iguana. That wasn't weird. In fact it was kind of cool. He mostly just stayed in his glass cage, but occasionally we would take him out to play. He was a friendly little lizard. Pete liked to talk about how long they could live and how big they could get. He was psyched to have his pet for the long haul. Plans to build him a big glass case were even under way.

Of course our house wasn't the best for keeping an exotic animal. The only source of heat in this sprawling house was a wood burning stove. Fired up and cooking, the stove could easily heat the whole house, but it was hard work keeping it fired up during the dead of winter.

One morning I woke up and the fire was almost out. The house was cold, really cold. I checked on the iguana. He was sleeping on his heated rock. I figured he was probably warmer than any of us. I went outside to chop up some wood.

It took a while to chop the wood and then load up the fire. By the time I got it roaring again, the house was freezing. I went into the kitchen at the far end of the house to start making coffee. Pete came running in, holding the limp iguana in his hands a few minutes later.

"Poor iguana. The heat stone broke and he froze to death last night." I consoled Pete and was about to offer to help dig a small grave when he took out a large zip lock bag and put the iguana in it. He zipped it up and then put the clear plastic bag, with the iguana clearly showing inside, into the freezer.

I just stood there for a second. I think I blinked a few times. When I had enough coffee for my mind to snap awake I turned to Pete. "Ummm, Pete? Why did you put a dead iguana in the freezer?"

"I'm going to save him in a jar with Formaldehyde, but I have to keep him frozen until I get it." He was just going to leave it at that. He was walking back to his room with his coffee. I had to stop him.

"Umm, what do you mean a jar? You're going to keep him?"

"Sure, I have a few others." Sure enough he went back to his room and brought out several jars. Two had snakes inside. The other had a rat. "This way I can keep them forever!"

I really couldn't respond. It seemed really strange, but that was Pete. Pete was strange. I just hoped that he would get that thing out of the freezer. Of course six months later the fun game to play on new visitors was to ask them to get something out of the freezer. Watching them jump ten feet when they see our frozen pet iguana was always a blast.

To this day I can't say I've ever met someone like Pete. He was 25 years old, and almost completely bald. Pete loved to talk, and did a good job of it. He seemed very smart, but when it came to making big decisions, he always went the wrong way. He had grown up in the Bronx and was a complete crack head by the time he was 20. He quit the crack, moved to the suburbs, and was now managing a KFC in Bridgeport. He even had a little moustache and goatee, exactly like Col. Saunders.

Lenny had worked at a KFC in Oregon, one of his many jobs, and worked with Pete for a few months in Mt. Kisco when he had moved back. When Pete got transferred, he wanted to stay in the area, so he found the house in Pound Ridge, about halfway between Kisco and Bridgeport. A few months after I moved in, Lenny suddenly had to move out due to legal reasons. He had just paid a month's rent, so he took his time moving out, and stopped by everyday even after he did. We lucked out in finding a new roommate, since Bob had been calling from Boston. He was looking to move back to New York, and a guy who lived down the road from us offered him a job painting. Pete and Bob had met a few times, but Pete thought he could get along with anyone. He was just happy that we wouldn't have to split a month's rent between the two of us.

Lenny had rented a place with Pete in Kisco, so we got to know each other pretty well. He knew I was a freak, and he kind of didn't get me, but he didn't care. When he didn't understand my way of life, he'd just say, "Oh well, musicians are weird." He was right. We are.

Bob was a great guitarist, who was very shy about playing. Hanging out in the pit, he would rip away, but refused to play when there was anyone around. Bob and I quickly became drinking buddies when he moved in. One of the best jams I've ever played in was when PJ came over, and I played bass while Bob and PJ traded solos back and forth. We played one blues tune for a half hour, and PJ loved it. I could see that he could do the whole jam band thing if he wanted.

One day Pete came home with a big surprise for Bob and me. He had been courting, and I do mean the traditional gifts for the family style of courting, a 15-year-old girl from El Salvador. Her whole family had worked for Pete at the Kisco KFC. It seemed that one of the girl's brothers had been either beating her, or trying to molest her or both. Her parents told her that if she reported him, they would send her away to live in El Salvador. That's when Pete offered to marry her.

Her parents happily signed the papers making Pete her official guardian. She was going to be moving in, and the wedding was going to be the next day with the justice of the peace, but they needed a witness. Bob looked horrified. I just took a hit from the bong and said, "Sure, why not?"

Party Time

The day before the party, we had a marathon jam session. We started at ten in the morning, and played until the sun went down. I was still refusing to use a pick, so my blisters had blisters. Holding my hand up to the light, I could swear I could see through my fingers. We were half way through our final song of the night, when suddenly I felt my bass strings get wet. This has happened before. I figured one of the blisters broke and the saline inside had covered the strings. I expected to look down and see just a loose flap of skin on my finger. It didn't really hurt at all, and in fact when it happened in the past, I could feel the strings better, and then play better. I just kept playing, keeping my eyes on PJ and Alex, trying to stay in time. PJ glanced over at me, and stopped playing immediately. I looked at Alex and he was staring at me. "What's up, did I fuck up?"

"Chuck, look at your bass.," Alex said calmly. I looked down to see the white pick guard on my bass covered in red. I looked down at my hand, and blood was pouring out of my index finger. The party was the next day. I started freaking a little, worried that I may not be able to play, but PJ was just laughing.

I wrapped my finger in my shirt to try to stop the bleeding. "What's so funny? Am I going to be able to play tomorrow with no index finger? I can't play with just my middle and ring fingers." I was just starting to feel a throbbing pain in my fingertip. It didn't seem like it was bleeding too much, but it hurt.

PJ just kept laughing. He threw me a pick and said, "Alex, go get him a band-aid, it looks like we have to practice some more, get Chuck used to playing with a pick." We played a few songs, and the pick wasn't slowing me down as much as I thought it would. The bass did sound a little muted with dried blood filling the ridges of the strings. I would have to boil them when I got home.

At the end of the practice PJ opened up his duffle bag and threw Alex and I each a tape. The cover had the familiar black and white photo of the two girls touching tongues. The picture was clear in the middle, but got fuzzy as it went to the edges. In big green letters at the top it said

"The Presstones." On the bottom, in smaller green letters was "Harmful or Fatal if Swallowed."

My parents house was an old colonial on top of a hill, at the end of a dead end road. We were neighbored on two sides by forest, enough forest to last a childhood. We had a running feud with the only actual house bordering us. Across the street was the Bennet Cerf Estate. He had died, and his wife now owned the property. It was the only estate left on that side of town; everything else had been subdivided in a push of suburban sprawl. They had a two-hole golf course, clay tennis court, and a river that lead into the woods that we shared as neighbors. Since the Widow Serf and her new husband, Mayor Wagner, were only there on weekends in the summer, and I was friends with the children of the staff, I had a free reign of their property throughout my childhood.

Our driveway used to snake around to a small garage in the back yard, but we had built an addition halfway up the driveway, and the old garage was now in the middle of a nice green lawn. The lawn had acted as a wiffle ball field, croquet lawn, football field, shooting range, dog pooping area, bird feeding area (never while as a shooting range), and tent city during the memorable week long party the year before. This party would be a little more refined. My brother still talks to everyone he has ever met, and a bunch of them from college and high school would be there, but so would the whole family, and the family of his girlfriend. So there would be a keg, but there would also be a beautifully catered (by dear ole mom) spread, and a bunch of stuff from the bakery where Rebecca worked. This was also the first time there was going to be a band.

We set up in front of the old garage, so there was plenty of power, and Alex could have his drums on a concrete floor. PJ and I set up our amps, out towards the woods, hitting a good part of the party, but allowing those who just wanted background music to sit on the back porch of the house in relative peace. We threw a garbage can lid in the middle of us for cigarettes. This would be the first time we could ever smoke and play at the same time. My brother had set up the stereo, and had 600,000 CD's, so everyone was picking out music to play before we got started.

If I Had Wings These Windmills Would Be Dead

Alex, PJ and I were in the front of the house going over last minute details. Alex's girlfriend had set up a sign up sheet for people who wanted to be on a mailing list. We were even going for e-mail addresses; the Internet was the next big thing. My fingertip was taped back on, but I would have to play with a pick. When there were finally enough cars to line as far down the street as you could see, we walked to the back yard and got ready.

We had come up with a little warm up tune one day when Alex was late to practice. He took us out to his truck, lifted the hood and said, "Have you ever seen a manifold glow?" and we had the name of a song. We would start off with that, and then go into the Presstones theme. From the moment we started, the pick just felt right. It gave a much crisper sound than I usually had. I was afraid it would slow me down, but if anything I felt a little quicker. I looked out over the party, and there were a lot of people there, but I knew every one of them. I had told stories to, joked with, drank with, sang badly with all of them. My brother is only two years older than me, so our friends had been more inter-connected as the years went on. I had spent a semester at Hobart with my Bro, and partied at his frat house with all of his friends from up there.

We ripped through a bunch of songs, and it felt too easy. PJ's guitar was ripping, and Alex had his unraveling cymbal shaking and grooving while he was pounding out the beats. Even the eldest people there seemed to like it. We definitely had a throwback sound.

Suddenly, just as we finished one song, my father jumped in and yelled "Congratulations, the cops came. Our neighbors called a noise complaint, the cops came, and they said 'you sound great, keep playing' and left." Everyone cheered at that.

"That's the first time the cops ever came here for a party and my parents were home," I yelled, and got laughs from everyone but my parents. When we got to Pomp and Circumstance, no one could find Jacky; he finally came out of the house and began his speech. We put down our instruments as he spoke, so that we could take a bit of a set break. He gave a speech thanking family, teachers and friends.

PJ and I both started pounding down beers. I felt great, but I asked him with uncertainty how he thought we sounded. "Well, you see why I've been telling you to play with a pick. That's how you're supposed to play these songs."

"I guess, but when my finger heals, I'm still going to play a bunch of the tunes without it."

"Just make sure you use it in the right songs," That's all he said. We both started mingling, and talking to people before playing again. Everyone seemed to like it. Most said to me that they didn't even know I played an instrument, and that the band was great.

When I saw Alex and his girlfriend, they looked at me with big smiles and she said "We got names from Boston to DC here on the mailing list. These people came from all over." Alex and I looked at each other thinking the same thing. Tour.

We played the rest of our songs, and it went as well as we could hope. When we finished people kept yelling for more, but we had played all of our songs. PJ just looked at me and said, "Follow me." He started playing some simple chord changes, and when Alex and I joined in, he started ripping it up. We played a couple of improv (although I'm sure they weren't improv to PJ) tunes, and a couple of tunes we had already played. When we finally finished, it seemed everyone loved it. A girl I hadn't seen since high school came running up to me asking us to play her birthday in a couple of weeks. I got her number, and then got a beer.

Alex's girlfriend had collected names of people who weren't even there, but whose friends thought they would like it. We sold most of the tapes we had brought. PJ and Alex didn't stay too late, but the party lasted late into the night. Most of the family had left, and a nice campfire was built in the middle of the back lawn. A few tents were set up for people staying overnight, and a few of my brother's friends were sitting around playing guitars. I joined them for a few tunes, but my fingers were shot, so I sat back and enjoyed just listening. I was a little drunk, a little high, and a whole lot satisfied with my day. The only problem was the fact that Rich never showed up. I had left a message, asking him to come, but I guess it would take him awhile.

Sunrise

The Butcher and the Baker was an awesome bar. It was a decent restaurant. It was more convenient than anything else. It was right next to the movie theater on the Bedford Green. In middle school it was the perfect date spot after going to see Footloose on a Saturday afternoon. Years later it would just become the perfect bar.

It was the closest bar to the house in the woods where I was living. When Lenny lived there we didn't hit the bars very often, but after he moved out and Bob moved in, the Butcher became a second home. Especially when our other roommate, Pete, married a 15 year old girl from El Salvador and she moved in. It was a huge house. They kind of had their own wing, so we didn't even see her that often, but it was still weird, so we went out a lot.

The bartenders were both great. It was either Chris, a kid we went to school with who gave us lots of free drinks, or Kate, a woman I thought was cool because she always made us sandwiches when the fresh bread came in the early morning hours. They had a sit down Miss Pac-man table, and for a quarter you could listen to a 45 minute long "Mountain Jam" by the Allman Brothers on the juke box.

There was a great revolving cast of characters in and out of the place every night, and Bob and I came up with names for everyone, even if we knew their name already. There was one guy with really creepy eyes. He would stare a hole into any good looking girl in the bar. Bob said he looked like a stalker. One day we were eating lunch at the house. We both looked at the last celery stick on the plate. In unison we shouted. "Celery! That's his name!" So the creepy eyed guy became known as Celery.

There was another girl who was pretty cute and really nice; she just never had any facial expression of any kind. One night she told us she had won a lot of money in the lottery as she bought us drinks. A week later she told us her good friend had died as we bought her drinks. Both nights she had the exact same facial expression. We joked that sex with her would be a lot of work. Finally you would have to ask her if she came yet. "She'd be like, 'yes, seven times. That was the best sex ever.' in the same bland voice."

Chuck Howe

"Yeah she is muy Blando,"

We again shouted in unison, "Blando Calrissian!"

It would have been the perfect nickname too, if we hadn't let it slip to someone else. Years later I was at a Maceo Parker show and ran into her. "So, Blando Calrissian huh?" was the first thing she said.

"Umm," I tried to think quickly, but I was busted and I knew it. "You just never smiled, I'm sure you have a beautiful smile."

For the first time ever I could read her face. "Fuck off Chuck" is what it told me.

Carl was the Maitre d' at a high end local restaurant. He was really friendly and happy and loved everyone, because he was shit face hammered 90 percent of the time. He became known as Road Soder, because every time he left the bar he would ask for a "Road Soder." Chris would pour an Orange Stoli and Cranberry juice, a drink we called the Rat Bastard, into a paper cup for him to take on the road. A double would be a Calvin Coolidge Rat Bastard. Road Soder almost got away with his blatant public intoxication until one night, Road Soder in hand; he crashed into and almost destroyed the 300 year old well on the Bedford Green. It was literally 100 feet from the bar. How he got going fast enough to almost destroy a stone well, I will never know.

We were at the bar most nights, and Bob and I saw the sunrise from the barstools more often than I should admit. We were smart enough to head home once the sun was out. More often than not we would get home, smoke a joint and either sing doo-wop or I would sing songs about eating road kill while Bob played the guitar until Pete's wife came out to catch her school bus.

Sing Sing

My fingers were almost healed by Katie's party, but I still used a pick for most of the songs. It seemed we had a much bigger set list, so I felt better than I had at my brother's party. I knew some of the people there, but Katie was a year older than my brother, and I didn't know her that well. I was sure she had a lot of friends I had never met.

She lived with her sister in Ossining (home of the famous Sing Sing Prison), in a cool little house in a multi-ethnic residential area. From her front porch you could see the Tappan Zee Bridge and the Hudson River off in the distance. We were going to set up in the back yard. They lived at the corner of an intersection, so there would be fences on two sides, and small open yards on two sides. Katie assured us that the nearest neighbors had been invited, and our playing would be no problem. Again we were setting up to play in the late afternoon, so we would be done before it got too late.

PJ and his wife came with a friend, Maria, who worked with Lucy in Greenwich. All three seemed to be in an especially good mood. Alex showed up a little later, but his girlfriend couldn't make it. She was at a job interview in the city.

We set up quickly, as clouds began to gather in the sky. If it rained we were screwed. PJ would electrocute himself with his ancient guitar and amp. All three of us had a lot more confidence this time around. We knew that we would blow them away. Before we set up everyone was asking what type of music we played, and curiosity was growing. My brother showed up right as we were about to start playing. He and Katie were just about the only people I recognized, but I almost felt better, like what did I have to prove to any of these people, as long as PJ thought it went well, nothing else really mattered.

We ripped into a good hour-long set of tunes. The minute we began people perked up and started listening. They were hooting and hollering at the end of the tunes. Neighbors walking down the street stopped and stayed to listen. Everyone was dancing and drinking, and a lot looser than they were at my brother's party. It felt great.

As we neared the end of our first set, Katie and her sister began yelling for us to play "Closer to Fine" by the Indigo Girls so they could sing it. We hadn't planned on this happening, and I didn't even know if PJ had ever heard the song. I knew it, but had never tried playing it. PJ just jumped into the final song of the set, but when we finished they kept yelling for Closer to Fine.

"I tell you what," PJ yelled over the party. We didn't have a singer, so we had no microphone. "Let us take a quick break, and when we come back we'll play it if you can sing it." PJ put his guitar down, and ran inside for a bathroom break.

I went and got another beer. My hands were shaking with adrenaline, and I needed a drink and a smoke to steady myself. Everyone was patting me on the back and saying how great it sounded. A few people introduced themselves as people I knew back in elementary school. I recognized the names, but not the faces. After a few minutes, PJ found me and pulled me over to our setup.

"OK, it's an easy song. There's a change for the chorus, and a bridge. Here, I'll show you." He quickly ripped out the tune. Alex sat listening, and I was gently fingering my strings, planning a simple little bass line for it. When it looked like we got it, PJ yelled out to turn the stereo off, and we pulled up Katie. She and a group of her friends all sang out the lyrics as we played the song. We started the chorus while they were still singing verses and they forgot the words at one point, but they got the whole party singing and it turned into a great way to start a set.

Our second set was a little different than the first. In the first set, we stuck to the surf tunes. Second set we would play more of our Latin tunes and our longer ballad. A few drops had fallen, but the feared rain stayed away. It was just getting dark as we finished our set. We stayed and drank for a while, but PJ pulled me aside a little later.

"Hey, can we go back to your place in a bit. Lucy and her friend kind of want to smoke some pot," PJ seemed a little uncomfortable bringing it up. "I could grab some beers on the way, too." PJ actually didn't live too far from my house in Pound Ridge. The problem was getting there. Ossining was far, and we had all drank a little too much already. PJ looked really excited. "I think my wife likes her new friend. I may end up having a little threesome at some point. This is so cool." He was acting his age, which was a lot younger than he normally acted.

"Yeah, sure, why not?" I really didn't know anyone at the party, and had no real urge to stay. Rebecca was working, and then had some schoolwork to finish up, so she wasn't coming by. So I led PJ and his wife through Westchester, back across to Pound Ridge.

We smoked and drank hard when we got to my place. Lucy seemed really sweet. She reminded me of a lot of the hippy chicks I met on tour, but she had a deeper wisdom in her eyes. Maria wasn't really remarkable in any way. She looked pretty fucked up, and didn't say much. She was just staring at Lucy and PJ the whole time. We were all smiles when PJ and the girls left. We had played well and we knew it. We had sold a lot more tapes, and got a lot more names for a mailing list.

Shortly after they left my phone rang. It was Steve; the Dead had just announced tour dates for the northeast. He was planning on a good two-week stretch, and wanted to know if I would go with him. I couldn't think of a reason why not, so I signed up to go. It had been a great night...

Pete and his wife woke up at six every morning. She would shower, and get ready, and then Pete would drive her to school several towns away. This would not be a problem, if she didn't blast Michael Jackson from the time she got up until she left. Bob was pissed.

Most nights Rebecca would come over for dinner, and do her homework on the loft. When she finished, we would hang out for a bit, and she would usually fall asleep by nine. That's when Bob and I would go out. When we got home, I would smoke, we would play some music, and then I'd go into my room and wake her up. We'd snuggle until she headed home in the early morning so her mom didn't know she was out all night. It was the perfect situation for me; I don't know how healthy it was for her.

I had missed the rehearsal following Katie's party. My car had died en-route, and it being the time before cell phones were just for crack dealers, PJ and Alex were left standing around in Alex's basement. My car was still in the shop, so PJ picked me up for our next practice. He was pissed from the moment he pulled up. It was not just at me for missing the last practice, but he didn't want to talk about it. We got to Alex's and there was no one there. We waited for an hour, chain smoking in the driveway, but no one came, not even Alex's brother. Finally we jumped back in PJ's car and went back to my house. We stopped at a store on the way so PJ could pick up a sixer of Rheingold. It was cheap beer, but it was his favorite.

"You should have offered Alex the room here when Lenny moved out," This was the first time anyone had mentioned anything about it. PJ had already downed two of the beers, and was starting to talk fast. Bob wasn't home, and Pete and his wife were back in Pete's room. He had just bought a TV the size of some European countries, so we never saw them anymore. "His parents have been fighting nonstop, and he needs to get out of there. He probably didn't want to go home after class. I don't know why he would blow it off." He paused and looked right at me, "Well, now you know how it feels."

I had apologized for missing practice, but I could tell PJ took it a little personally. "I never even thought of it. I've told him we could practice here, but he says he wants to keep his drums at home." I thought about it for a minute. "There's room here. If he wants to get out he could stay here a bit." Bob would be pissed, but I had to offer.

"Well, we'll see when we talk to him. Grab me another beer."

PJ stayed for a while, and didn't seem to be in any rush to get home, which was odd. Shortly after he left Alex called. He apologized up and down for missing practice. He got caught in the city. He and his girlfriend had found a place, and were signing the lease. He swore up and down that we would still get together at his parents place to play. I offered my house again, and he seemed to think about it. He would get back in touch. He still had to call PJ. When I told him I'd be going on Dead tour for two weeks he seemed more relieved than pissed. This threw warning signs up for me. I figured it meant the end of the Presstones.

Merde d'Jour

The Dead tour had been a disaster. We spent every cent we had made to get one of our buddies out of jail. We would get the money back when he went to trial, but it still stung. Returning home was no better.

Bob, who was very fickle about living situations, had enough of living with Pete and his wife. She had started her summer vacation, and was home blasting Michael Jackson all day long. The day I got back, Pete informed me that his mother, grandmother, Uncle and their parrot were coming up from the Bronx for the weekend. The kicker was that the uncle was an extreme heroin addict. Pete assured me that he would be fine; he would just nod off a lot, and go into the bathroom a lot. This tipped Bob over the edge. He basically started packing his bags then and there.

I called Alex, but his answering machine picked up. I left a message letting him know that I was back. If he wanted to set up his drums in the loft, it would be fine. Then I called PJ, and I could tell he was down the moment he picked up. He said he had left a few messages for Alex, but he hadn't called back. It was understandable. The move to the city must have been hectic. PJ told me that he was in the middle of something, and he'd call me back the next day.

Then I called Rebecca. At least she seemed happy to hear from me. The moment she heard my voice, she asked if she could come over. I said sure, then went to the pit, turned on the TV, and packed a bowl. She wouldn't be there for at least a half an hour. After a few minutes Bob came in and grabbed the pipe. It was rare for him.

"I found a place in Kisco. It's a little studio, but I think it'll be perfect," I had no idea how he had found a new place. He hadn't left since I got home. "I've been looking for the last week. I just can't stand this place anymore." The music hadn't bothered me much, but Bob was very sensitive about his sleep and how he is woken up. Jacko wasn't doing it for him. I was pissed that my rent would end up going up, but I couldn't really blame Bob.

Rebecca was late in getting there, and when she finally pulled up she came running in crying. "Rebecca what's wrong?"

"I need to use your phone. I hit the dirt road, and it was raining, and my car just spun and hit a stonewall. The front is all dented." I gave her the phone and went outside to take a look. Sure enough, the front passenger corner was dented in. The headlight had shattered, and the bumper and side were pushed in. It was a brand new car, and Rebecca had been working hard to keep up with the payments. The damage wasn't horrible, but it would be expensive...

It wasn't a very good week for anyone. Bob was fed up with the situation. He figured with three guys in the house it would be fun, but throw in a young bride for one of the guys, and a girlfriend who was over all the time for the other, and it was not what he had bargained for. He finally told Pete that he would be moving out at the end of the month, and Pete understood. Pete and I were trying to figure out what we would do when the phone rang.

"Hey Chuck, its Alex." I hadn't heard from him since getting back from tour. I knew he was a little pissed off at me for missing two weeks, and I assumed from what PJ had said that he was pissed that I hadn't asked him to move into the house.

"Hey Alex. I was wondering when I'd hear back." I had left a few messages, and I was sure that PJ had called him at least once a day. "Did you talk to PJ yet?

"No, I thought I'd call you first," I didn't like the sound of that. "Well, between work, and moving in to the new place, and spending time with my girlfriend..." I cut him off before he could finish. I had been afraid of it all along.

"You're not going to be able to come up to play too much."

"Yeah. I guess we're going to take a bit of a break. Maybe once I get settled..." I don't really remember the rest of the conversation. He was asking about PJ, and I think I just told him to call PJ. I sat down and grabbed a bottle of Jack from the cabinet. That was it. I was sure of it. Alex would be on the phone with PJ for a while, but the next time the phone rang I knew it would be PJ. Sure enough, five minutes later the phone rang.

Well today has been the worst day of my life," I expected PJ to have

If I Had Wings These Windmills Would Be Dead

been pissed, but he was overdoing it a little. "Alex's phone call was just the topper."

"Oh shit, what happened?" I expected to hear that a family member was sick or something, but instead I got the bombshell.

"My wife is leaving me for that bitch she brought to the party. They are moving to San Francisco next week." PJ had an obvious slur to his voice. He had been drinking hard already. "She's even taking the fucking cat."

"With who? Maria?" I was a little surprised, but not really. "What are you going to do?"

"Yeah, my wife is running off with Maria," he said it out loud almost as if to convince himself. "I don't know what I'm going to do man. We got the rent paid here until the end of the month. She already moved to her parents, until they take off for the West."

"Dude, Bob is moving out at the end of the month, you could start moving stuff over here whenever you want." Pete was walking past the pit to the kitchen right as I said that.

"Who's moving in now?" Pete said in his booming Bronx accent.

"It's PJ. He needs a place."

"Oh, OK. He can move in. I like him." Pete had only met him once or twice, but they were both big talkers, and got into good deep conversations both time.

"You hear that. You got a place." I was feeling like shit because the band was done, I could only imagine how PJ felt. I was hoping that knowing he had a place to go would at least make him feel a little better.

"OK, but it would probably be for a couple of months only. I'll probably move back to the city at some point. I can't really just leave my job." I could tell he was already forming a new plan. His whole plan for life was just turned upside down, and he already had a new plan in place.

"As long as you need it. And if you need any help moving."

Curried Eggs and National Steel

PJ's move consisted of two trips. On his first trip he brought boxes of cassettes and CD's, one suitcase of clothing, and his guitars. With the Presstones he only played two different guitars. One was the red Hollow body Gibson that he used for most of the songs. The other was a Danelectro.

The Danelectro was a guitar from Sears back in the 60's. The body was made out of cheap plywood, but it was painted with red glitter paint to give it a flashy appearance. The pick-ups were the signature piece. They were made out of old Sears Lipstick tubes. The originals were only made for a few years, but a new company came out in the early nineties selling even cheaper reproductions; unfortunately for them they never got the rights to the name Danelectro, and were soon run out of business.

He had at least 6 more guitars. One was a national Steel Resonator Guitar that had a bright steel plate that helped give it a real tinny sound. He had a lap steel that he would pull out every now and then, and a beautiful twelve string. My favorite by far became the tenor guitar.

It was a roughly hand made four string acoustic guitar. It was basically the exact opposite of a bass. The tuning pegs were just knife carved hard wood spikes. The strings were real gut, made now out of sheep intestines instead of the "Cat Gut" they used to use. The neck was very thin, yet completely straight. The body was a triangle with curved sides made out of very roughly hand cut wood. It was the most redneck thing I had ever seen, and I fell in love with it instantly. Though we didn't have the band together anymore, we would jam very often, and on occasion I would play the tenor while PJ jammed on the Resonator. As much as the Presstones would teach me about the whole surf genre, living with PJ I'd learn more about Jazz, Tin Pan, Jug Band Music and Bluegrass than I thought possible.

I had sold Django Reinhardt albums at the music store before, but had never listened to a single thing. PJ told me about how he was a gypsy, and as a child his carriage had caught fire, and he badly burned his left hand saving his guitar. While his fingers were still smoking he wrapped them together in twos, where they healed together to form a claw hand with only "two" fingers. He then grew up to be better than any guitarist alive with all of his or her fingers. During World War II, when most of the Parisian musicians fled to England, The Gypsy Django remained in Paris, playing every night. PJ had old Hot Club albums that he had done with Stephane Grappelli before the war that blew my mind. Apparently Reinhardt would not forgive Grappelli for leaving Paris during the war, but the two ended up meeting again years later; before Django died he forgave his old partner.

He wouldn't just teach me about music. His second trip contained all of his books, from Woodhouse to the graphic novel Maus. He had an extensive collection that I got to read like a library. The rest of the second trip consisted of boxes of vinyl, a sleeping bag and a sleeping pad, and a bike. That was it. He was done with his move. It seemed like he had more guitars than clothes.

For his first night in the house, he went out and bought some groceries, and made all of us curried eggs, stuffed grape leaves, and a huge salad. The guy could cook, too. Some of the foods he made were great, but I never even tried the pickled herring and onion sandwiches. The smell alone was too much. But he did introduce me to El Pico, Cafe Bustello and the so-called Spanish coffees. Call me crazy but I still prefer to make my espresso with a 1.99 pound of El Pico, instead of the 17.99 a pound they charge for fresh espresso beans at the coffee shops.

Living with PJ was going to be a trip. Some mornings before I went to sleep, PJ would wake up and say something like, "I'm going to pick up some shark tonight. You want to throw 5 bucks in?" I never knew what he was talking about, but I'd throw in five bucks, and get a great meal that night. Pete, aside from the fact he was working at KFC, was a pretty good cook himself, and though he rarely ate with us, he'd always talk with PJ and try to figure out what he was making. PJ always invited Pete and his wife to eat with us, but they always declined. They were newlyweds after all, and spent most of their time together and would usually eat much earlier than we did.

After Bob moved out, but before PJ really moved in, Pete's family came and stayed for the weekend. His mother was in her late fifties but

If I Had Wings These Windmills Would Be Dead

looked and acted like she was much older. Pete's grandmother looked absolutely ancient. His uncle was one of the scariest looking humans I had ever seen. He was bald, and grossly overweight. He would froth and spit when he talked. The whole weekend the only thing he ever wore was a white wife beater t-shirt, and a pair of stripped boxers. He had track marks all over his arms and legs from years of abuse. Some had healed. Some had been infected. It was just disgusting. I really wanted to leave, and Pete told me he would look after everything, but I really didn't want to leave this guy in a house with my stuff.

Sure enough almost every hour he would go to the bathroom for long stretches. He would fall asleep in the middle of a sentence. Meanwhile Pete's mother and grandmother did nothing but sit around the kitchen table, smoking cigarettes and drinking coffee. At first when I went to get a drink I thought my eyes were deceiving me. Pete's mother was handing his grandmother a packed pipe, and there was a small, easily recognizable dime bag of Bronx pot on the table. Pete's grandmother took a long hit and passed it to his mother. Pete was smiling at me.

"Oh yeah, I didn't tell you. They've been tokers for years." Pete was laughing at my obviously startled expression.

Pete's mother corrected him, "I've been smoking for years, Grandma just started about twenty years ago." Grandma just sat there smiling, with her hand out waiting for her turn. "I go down to the record store and buy a bag every day. The guy there loves me." Her brother woke from his sleep, looked around a bit, and then fell back to sleep. Pete being a crack head as a teen made a little more sense after that. He and his uncle weren't smoking any of the pot; it was just the mother and grandmother. I had a sudden desire to pack a bowl of really good pot for them.

When I came back with the bag, the mother took one look and said, "Oh no. We don't want any of that. We've had that stuff before; it's too hard for us." I could understand that. If you smoked the brown Bronx your whole life, and then suddenly got a hold of good pot, they probably thought it was laced with something.

The day they left, PJ moved in. It was a lot of fun while it lasted. He would tell me a story about some musician, and then play me an album.

I'd tell him about some show I went to and play him a tune or two. We jammed a lot too. Sometimes just the two of us, and sometimes whoever happened to be over would join in.

Eventually Rich came over for a lesson. PJ had been going to Rich's house since he moved in. It was the first time I had talked with him since he left the pit all pissed off. We spoke only briefly the first time, and then he and PJ went up to the loft for the lesson. By the third time he came over we talked a little more, until finally he stayed for a beer and a bowl after one of his lessons. After that we were always friendly toward one another, but never close friends again.

PJ and I both stayed in the house for a couple of months, but soon he wanted to go back to the city, and I didn't want to stay there through the winter. Pete had a few friends in the area who were looking for places, so it was going to work out for all of us. On one of our last days in the house the phone rang. PJ picked up, and was on for a long time before handing me the phone. I was surprised to hear Alex's voice on the other end of the line.

"Hey Alex, what's going on?" I hadn't talked to him since the night he said he wasn't going to be able to play anymore. I figured PJ had been on the phone with his brother, or parents, so I didn't hear any of his conversation with Alex.

"Well, my girlfriend and I split up." I immediately thought he was moving back up and wanted to start playing again. Unfortunately PJ was about to move to the city. "I'm up at my parents tonight, but I leave tomorrow."

"You leave? Where are you headed?" With Alex, I had no clue. He always seemed to have some plan in his head. I could only imagine what it was this time.

"I joined the Navy. I signed up for a five year enlistment. I leave for basic training in the morning," I was actually surprised by this. It was the last thing I expected Alex to say, so it should have been expected. "I'm going to play in a Navy band, and learn electronics. I think it's exactly what I need."

"OK Alex. If it's what you want. You're sure you're not just overreacting to the break up?"

If I Had Wings These Windmills Would Be Dead

"Oh, I probably am, but there are worse things I could have done. I could have started drinking again." That was true, but by the next time I saw him he would be in the Navy and drinking.

"I guess we'll have to wait five years for a Presstones reunion. Good luck in the Navy." That was it as far as I was concerned. PJ was going to the city. Alex was going down south somewhere, and I was going to be up in Kisco. The band was done.

After PJ moved into the city, I kept in touch with him pretty often. He got back together with his jug band Pork Chop, and I went down to the Sidewalk Cafe to see them play once. Their version of Prince's Purple Rain was unbelievable. He was giving lessons, and playing in the subways. He was now a full time musician, which was what he should have been all along.

I moved back to Kisco and started working at a local coffee shop. Rebecca and I soon fizzled out. Maybe it was actually living close to each other, or just that we were going in different directions in our lives. It wasn't a bad break up, but it was a break up. I didn't really mind: I was distracted by all the women that populated the coffee shop.

Cindy

Every day at 5 she was outside. Sitting on the bench. Smoking a cigarette. She worked next door at the hair salon. I sat behind the counter looking out at her as I worked the espresso machine. I wanted nothing more than to walk outside. Sit next to her on the bench. Light a cigarette and start talking. If I could only talk to her I could get her to want me the way that I wanted her. But she was only ever outside at 5, when I had a late day rush of customers.

She came into the coffee shop once, with three of her friends from the salon. We were really busy and I didn't get to talk to her at all, but I did hear one of her friends call her Cindy. At least I had a name.

Cindy was never out on the bench on Wednesdays or Sundays. Those were my least favorite days. Then came one magical day. The owner was in the coffee shop and it was a slow afternoon. He asked me to go outside and sweep the sidewalk. He would look after the place. It was 4:58. Just as I got the broom I could see Cindy sitting down at the bench through the window. I hurried up and went outside.

I started sweeping right next to the bench immediately. She turned and looked at me as I started. She gave me a very sweet little smile. Her green eyes sparkled. I awkwardly blurted out, "Hi, my name is Chuck, I work here," as if to let her know I didn't just sweep the sidewalk for a living. I was immediately embarrassed, but at least I broke the ice. This was going to be the beginning. Right here...

"Haaaiu, my name is Cindy tehehe..." Her voice was like nails on a chalkboard or an overinflated balloon being rubbed by weak child hands. I was not expecting it at all. In my mind she was sweet and smart and funny and perfect in every way. It was OK, so her voice was a little abrasive. There was still a chance she was sweet and smart and funny. I noticed a text book in her lap.

"What are you reading?" I asked, hopeful that it might be a great physics or philosophy book.

"I'm supposed to go to school tonight, but I don't have a brain in my head." I finished sweeping and went inside without another word. After that I never noticed when it was five o'clock again.

Because We Have a Fucking Gig Tonight

"Hey Chuck, Merry Christmas."

"Merry Christmas to you too, Mugsy, how have you been?" It had been a few months since I heard from Mugsy; it was sort of weird for him to be calling at 11 in the morning on Christmas Day.

"I'm doing great. I have a new band with Butch." Mugsy, Butch and I had been in a band together a few years earlier. "It's kind of a heavy metal/hard core thing. We have a couple of mellow tunes too, you know, we try to change it up a bit. You'd like it." It didn't sound like anything I would like. I was really into James Brown and Parliament/Funkadelic at the time. "We have a gig on December 30th at O'Hurly's."

"Cool. I'll try to make it." I wasn't going to try too hard. Heavy metal just wasn't my thing.

"Actually, I'm calling because we need a bass player."

I hadn't played with a band in a while, and learning a bands entire catalog in 5 days sounded like a fun challenge. Before I knew I blurted out, "OK. I'll do it."

We practiced every night leading up to the gig, which was good because I needed it. The music was really fast and frantic, not what I was used to playing. But by the time we got to gig night I had all the tunes down. I didn't think I would, but I actually liked the music; we had the potential to be a good band.

I barely knew the drummer, Jimmy, but we practiced at his house. The lead guitarist, Gus, wrote most of the music and was really good. I didn't know him well, but I had always liked him back in high school. Always a nice guy. Kind of a quiet, office worker guy. Not really the type you would expect to find rocking out on the weekend in a band. Mugsy was the singer, and Butch was the rhythm guitarist. Both of them you would fully expect to be in a heavy metal band. And I was the little funky hippy bassist. We were a perfect band.

Butch wasn't allowed to drive. The state of New York had made that very clear. So I picked up him and Mugsy on gig day. I went to Mugsy's first and he came running down to the car all pumped up screaming, "We have a fucking gig tonight!"

"Yeah man. We have a fucking gig!" I am easily worked up, and he got me worked up real quick. By the time we got to Butch's house I was seven types of pumped. Butch came running out with his guitar and amp. Mugsy and I screamed in unison. "Hurry the fuck up. Because we have a fucking gig tonight!"

Everything became "because we have a fucking gig tonight." Get in the car because we have a fucking gig tonight. Should we get some coffee because we have a fucking gig tonight? Let's make sure we have enough blank tape to tape our gig tonight because we have a fucking gig tonight. So we went into town to get fucking cassettes and fucking coffee because we had a fucking gig.

Driving in my sleepy suburban town I suddenly felt the need to drive up on the sidewalks to take the inside turn and cut off the guy in front of me. I almost crashed ten times in about 5 blocks. I found head in parking in front of the coffee shop. Most spaces, you could pull forward and right out of the space. A few had signs in front, and you had to back out of the space and drive around.

There was a long line at the coffee shop but since I worked there, I knew I could slip in and pour us three coffees quickly. So Mugsy went to the record store for blank cassettes while Butch helped me with the coffee. I was just finishing pouring them when Mugsy came in with the tapes. As he came in he briefly talked to some guy at the back of the line. I had never seen him before.

I brought Mugsy his coffee; he is well over six feet tall and announced in a loud enough voice for every person in the shop to hear, "Hey Chuck, this guy over here says you drive like an asshole." He pointed to the guy who he talked to.

"Well tell that guy that I am an asshole. Because I have a fucking gig tonight."

"Yeah, that's what I told him. That you are an asshole and we have a fucking gig tonight."

If I Had Wings These Windmills Would Be Dead

Of course when I got to the car, I forgot I parked in a space with a sign in front of it, and didn't see the sign, so I just pulled forward, completely running over and crushing it. I could see everyone in the coffee shop looking out at me thinking, "Yes, he does drive like an asshole."

By the time we started playing, the place was packed. Kids were home from college, and everyone in the band hung out with a different crowd. Most knew one another; it was just rare to get everyone out at the same place. We expected a big turnout, but this was well beyond expectations.

We were even more surprised when we started playing. Our first song was a real thrasher, and the entire bar just started slamming. It was a big bar and was packed. People were throwing elbows and wrecking each other inches in front of us. There was no stage. We were right there in the thick of it. I started having to throw some elbows while playing, just to hold my ground. At one point Mugsy bumped into me. When we practiced at Jimmy's, we always had plenty of room. Mugsy must have thought I was one of the moshers, and gave me a hard hip check. I would have gone flying, but I hit a group of guys right next to us and they pin-balled me back to where I started.

We finished the first song and the crowd took a breath. Just as we started our second song, a bar back started walking across the room with a box of empty bottles. After a slow intro, we went right back to thrashing, and the crowd went right back to moshing. The bar back got slammed and the box of empties went flying. Bottles smashed everywhere, but everyone just kept dancing and we kept rocking. During the third song our instruments suddenly went silent. The crowd stopped mid slam. The owner came running up to us.

"You guys have to stop. It's too much. The place is going nuts, my employees are getting killed." Every one booed, but everyone stayed and kept drinking. We didn't even get to finish three songs and every person in the bar came up to me to say how awesome it was. We eventually packed up our gear and the owner came by and paid us the full amount for the night. Not bad for about 10 minutes of actual music. "When can you guys play again?"

The Sailor

Mugsy and I rented a shitty apartment right off the railroad tracks. Rich was still in town, and though we weren't really close anymore, we did hang out on several occasions. Rebecca and I had long split up, but I could tell he hadn't forgiven me. He knew I was running the coffee shop, and since it was such a hang out, he would show up all the time. I always went out of my way to welcome him in, but got a lukewarm reception at best.

It was shortly after Christmas when Rich walked into the shop in the middle of the day. The daytime was pretty slow, there were always nannies nursing their coffee and just hanging out, but very few customers that needed help. I had plenty of time. Rich was actually smiling as he walked in, and gave me a big hello.

"Hey Rich, what's up? I usually don't see you so early."

"Oh I've got a surprise for you. He was following me, where is he?" I couldn't see the parking lot from behind the counter, but Rich was looking out at it. His eyes got wide, "Here he is." A few seconds later Alex came walking in the door.

Alex looked as clean cut as I had ever seen him before. His hair had grown in, but was kept very short, especially on the sides. He hadn't grown at all, but he looked taller in his dark navy pea coat. His facial piercings were gone. The goatee and sideburns were gone too, but he had a neatly groomed mustache. Navy rules, no hair below the top lip. His face looked leaner, but you could still tell he was built like a tank under his jacket. I gave him a huge hug and led him in to the couch area.

I asked Garrett, my freaky co-worker, to make a couple espressos. When I handed one to Alex, he pulled out a silver flask, and poured a good shot and a half into the cup. He handed me the flask, and I poured a small shot into the back of my throat and swallowed. It was a really nice, smooth whiskey. "I guess you're not in AA anymore?"

"Na. I think it's impossible to be in the Navy and not drink. Hey, do you think you can find any acid? It's the only thing they don't test for."

I made a note to myself that this was a completely different Alex than I knew almost 2 years before. I had not even been around acid since the Dead Show in Oregon.

"Ask Steve when he's in next. He probably doesn't have it, but he knows where it is. So how long are you home?" Steve was a good friend of both of ours, and though he didn't smoke he made a lot of money selling buds on the couch of the place. He was one of those guys who can play five people at once in chess. I only played him a few times. He would toy with me, letting me think I was going to trap him, and then suddenly I would hear "Checkmate," and always the move before I would have him in checkmate. He was also a speed-reader. I had tested that plenty of times at late night high school parties.

"Cool. I can't wait to see him. Hey Rich, what were you saying about a gig?" Seeing Alex again, I had almost forgotten Rich was still there. While were no longer close at all, we had gotten to the point of being friendly again at least. We had seen each other play. He was getting better and better. He and a friend even opened for my heavy metal band once.

"Well, you know my buddy Dennis? Whose sister died?" I knew Maggie better than I knew Dennis. She was a brilliant violinist who had played with Yitzhak Perlman and Aretha Franklin. She had started a music school in Minnesota, where her husband, also a former classmate of mine, was working. One morning driving to work she hit ice, spun out and crashed. Rich and Dennis had bonded ever since, having both joined the unfortunate club of losing a sister too soon. "I think it would be good therapy to get him to play live. He's a pretty good guitarist, and he can sing a bit. I figure we can play at O'Hurly's."

I looked at Alex, excited. I hadn't played live since the heavy metal band more or less split up. I was living with Mugsy, and jamming late into the night with whatever musicians were around. "Do we have a place to practice once or twice?" As I asked, Alex was smiling nodding at me. I could tell there was something fun planned.

"We can jam tomorrow at my mom's, and then play tomorrow night."

"Oh, sure, as long as we can play together once."

If I Had Wings These Windmills Would Be Dead

"I got Guy and his band to play, we are just opening. We need like 7 songs." Rich seemed to have it all planned out. If all I needed to do was show up and play bass, no problem. I had done well with the heavy metal thing with little practice.

"Where's your mom live?" I asked Alex. I knew his parents were splitting last time I talked to him.

"Same place. She's there with my brother. My Dad is closer to downtown in Armonk." That's all he said, so I figured he'd fill me in later.

"Let's do it then."

Our practice day was both completely useful, and absolutely worthless. We jammed a bit. Named a bunch of tunes back and forth. Dennis was a good guitarist. I had known him a long time, but had never heard him play. Rich had gotten a lot better too, so they were able to trade licks back and forth. Mostly we were playing tunes we had heard our whole lives. Not Fade Away, So You Wanna be a Rock n Roll Star, things like that. It felt good to jam with Alex again, but in the small confines of his basement, the dueling guitarists mostly drowned us out.

The basement was completely cleaned out, the mannequins all gone. Alex's drum set, looking even older, was the only thing left. There was still furniture upstairs, but the house had that look that houses on the market always have. Someone could stop by to look at the house at any moment, so keep it neat.

We drank a whole lot. We smoked a whole lot too. By the end of the day, we didn't remember a thing we did or played all day. We were getting ready to head to O'hurly's when Dennis suddenly came up with an idea for a song. He started playing a Latin rhythm that was remarkably similar to Una Cita con Anita. Alex and I smiled at each other, and ripped it into something even closer to the old tune. Rich and Dennis as dueling guitarists almost filled in for PJ, but not close enough. Alex and I were immediately spot on again. I knew which drum he was going to hit before he hit, and he knew exactly where my bass was going.

We quickly packed up Dennis' old Land Rover, and hit the road to the bar. Rich jumped in Dennis' car, and Alex rode with me. It was only a ten-minute drive, but by the time we got to there we had already planned a Presstones reunion. I had PJ's number, and still spoke to him pretty regularly. At one point there was talk of me going down to Brooklyn twice a week to jam, but at that point I just couldn't commit to it. He was living in a small place with his brother right over the bridge in Brooklyn. In his own words, he was making enough to get by, not enough to enjoy it.

The only problem with getting him up there would be money. PJ made money whenever he played. He was worth whatever he made, but we would have to make sure it would be worth his while to come up. We more or less agreed to give him the majority of anything we made. I knew we could make something at O'Hurly's, but the owner there never paid as much as he said he would, even if we packed the place. Hell, we were going to be playing there that night for almost nothing.

We set up and met with the guys we were opening for. The guitarist, Guy, had opened for my old heavy metal band, but I didn't really know him too well. I knew his bassist, just because we were both bassists in a small town. The guy was mostly a coke dealer, but he wasn't even too good at that. Guy had always impressed me as a guitarist. At that point he mostly played hard rock, but a few years later we would start jamming, and I was able to get him to explore all sorts of music. He ended up being able to play everything from Herbie Hancock tunes, to Zappa, to old school bluegrass. Guy had a lot of friends who were coming, and we all hung out in different circles, so I figured the place would be pretty full. By the time we were set up and ready to go there was a nice sized crowd.

We zipped through our songs pretty smoothly. I was barely paying any attention to Rich and Dennis, and just having fun with Alex. We were having a blast. The Latin tune was great, and Rich, Dennis and I just kept trading solos back and forth, with Alex more or less soloing throughout. Our final tune was "So you wanna be a Rock and Roll Star" in which we included a nice long improvised jam. I hadn't done that in a long time, since most of the heavy metal stuff I had been doing was very technical, and left little room for improv. I enjoyed it, but didn't think I really did anything special. After we were done Guy came up to me telling me how much he loved it. I made sure Rich and Dennis weren't around when I said, "Wait a week or two, the drummer and I are going to play with our old guitarist here soon."

Reunion

I made it down to Brooklyn in record time. PJ's place was long and narrow, with a narrow living room/kitchen leading to two narrow bedrooms. We grabbed his guitars and amp, and loaded up my jeep. We were off to Westchester for two gigs in two days.

We went straight to Alex's, and after the usual greetings, we jumped right into playing. I took out a sheet, and wrote down each tune as we played it. We couldn't remember all of our tunes, but the ones we remembered, we had down. PJ had written a few new tunes, and we added a few classic surf tunes that we had never played in the past. We weren't really ready, but we were close enough. That night we would be playing at Soltera's, a small bar across the street from my coffee shop. They didn't usually have music on Friday's, but since I promised the owner we would bring people in, he said OK. Saturday night would be the bigger show at O'Hurly's. It was a dive bar, but I had told everyone I knew to come, and I was sure we could pack the place.

We set up quickly at Soltera's, and I ran across the street to the coffee shop, opened the door, and shouted, "Anyone over 21, or close enough not to get carded, come across to Soltera's. My band is starting in about 5 minutes." A group of girls got up and came with me. My friend Steve got up from the coach, where he had a great night selling eighths to all the kids hanging out, gathered a group and joined us. My brother lived right up the street, and he got a good group of his friends. He wasn't going to be around on Saturday, but didn't want to miss out.

The bar was a very comfortable, low lit; dark wood paneled room, and had great sound. From the first tune the owner and the bartender were grooving right along. PJ, Alex and I clicked like we had played our last show just a week before. We even remembered a few tunes while playing, and improved off of stuff we didn't really know. I had learned one great lesson from listening to our tapes for two years. I just had to play bass. I didn't have to get fancy. I could play nice and solid, and PJ would have all the room in the world to rip. As we progressed PJ noticed the change and quickly took advantage of the space I was giving him. As we finished one song, he slammed his guitar so hard three strings broke.

Alex and I didn't realize and began the next tune. It was a slow version of Blitzkrieg Bop by the Ramone's, and I had a real simple bass line planned. As PJ went to fix his guitar I almost stopped playing, but he motioned for me to keep going. Alex and I just locked in on each other, and went off. I started ripping up and down scales like I had never done before. Alex was riding his cymbal, and throwing in fills, getting more and more intense. I was just ripping away, not noticing anything when I heard a few yells and hollers. I hadn't even noticed everyone was clapping in beat. Some girl I had never seen before was dancing on a table with PJ. Alex and I funked it up a little, and the whole place was clapping and screaming. I have no idea how long Alex and I were going, but I was suddenly snapped back to the song by PJ's guitar. We jumped right into the tune, and people went nuts.

Afterward, PJ and I headed to my apartment and he said, "I think you proved that you and Alex can go off on your own for a bit tomorrow night. Maybe we'll throw out some curveballs." We got to my apartment, poured some whiskeys, and we drank until we passed out.

My alarm went off at 5:30. Running a coffee shop really sucked. Garrett would be in at 7:00, but I had to get the place open. I got up, put on my pants, and without even looking at the bathroom, jumped in my car and Dwe'ed (I didn't make up the word, just the spelling) to work. My apartment was a shit-hole twenty feet away from the railroad tracks in Bedford Hills. A month after Mugsy and I moved out, the place was given to a group that tore it down and built a homeless shelter in its place. I guess it wasn't even good enough for the homeless. But it was fine for us; we got to play music at all hours of the night.

Haywood and Pearl lived downstairs. They were a very cute old couple that had rented their apartment for 35 years. Heywood was a mechanic, and there were always extra cars parked in the driveway. As he got older he started doing most of his work at home. He knew Friday was my day off, so he was always nice enough not to start working until later on Friday. Even though Mugsy and I were both crazy twenty somethings who were up all night with various friends always coming and going, they loved us. As Heywood put it "You guys are much better than those crack heads that was here a few years ago."

If I Had Wings These Windmills Would Be Dead

"Every Sunday night we had a ritual of listening to Pearl and Haywood have sex. They would call each other's name so loud, we didn't even need to open the living room window to hear them, but we did anyway. Pretty soon everyone would come over, Mugsy and Butch would make sushi, and we'd drink the better part of the evening, and then turn off the stereo by 9:30. It would start with moans and the get progressively louder and faster. Before the climax, I would turn the stereo back on, so they wouldn't hear our cheers. They must have been at least 80, but they knew what it was all about.

I opened the shop without even opening my eyes. It had all become routine. When Garrett got in, I went to the office and passed out. When I woke up I finished my shift, and then called Alex. PJ was already there, and they had come up with a bunch of new tunes. I went straight over, and we jammed the afternoon away. Alex and PJ were pounding down beers the whole afternoon. I was still more of a smoker than a drinker, so I excused myself to roll a joint. It seemed Alex had been drinking every minute I had seen him since he got back, but at least he seemed to be a happy drunk. He did claim to have been raped by a fat girl on New Years, but we all saw him hitting on her earlier in the night. He probably wouldn't have said anything if Steve hadn't accidentally walked in on them. PJ and I probably weren't the best influence on him either. Both of us had been drinking whiskey like it was water, but I think Alex would have been pounding drinks without us.

I was a little concerned about the money situation. We made about 50 bucks at Soltera's, just leaving a tip jar out. Alex and I gave all of that to PJ. I told him we would probably make about 150 to 200 at O'Hurly's, and I knew we could but the owner, Roger, was notorious for trying to under pay bands. The trick was to get your own people at the door. I don't know why I didn't think of it before, but I suddenly realized I had the perfect doormen in my old heavy metal band. Mugsy and Butch were both big scary looking dudes. Butch was known and loved by everyone in town, but it was known he could get really violent if he got pissed off. I was never worried. I had known him since I was 8. He was the BA to my Hannibal when we used to play A-Team. I called Mugsy, and we were all set.

Chuck Howe

When we got to O'Hurly's to set up, the place was starting to fill up already. A group of nannies from the coffee shop were there, and Alex immediately started flirting with one of them. She was a cute redhead from out west. After we set up, Roger approached me a little unsure. He was looking at PJ's amp that seemed a little small; he was still using the Ampeg Gemini 2. When I came in with my old band we had a full soundboard, and we were way too loud.

"Chuck, you guys don't have a singer?"

"Nope, don't need one."

"And that amp is going to be loud enough?"

"It blows away Marshall Stacks."

He looked at me suspiciously. "OK. How long are you going to play?" I could tell he was a little unsure. He didn't care about the music; he cared about how much people were going to drink.

"Don't worry Roger; this is the best band I've ever come here with. Everyone will get nice and drunk and have a good time, and buy lots of beer. You'll see." Before we got started I went and saw Butch at the door. "How's it going?" It was still early, but a lot would be off my mind if I knew we already made a bunch of money.

"We're doing OK, but once you guys start playing people will pack the place." Butch flashed me a stack of bills. I felt better. At least PJ would make more than he would playing in the subway for a couple of hours. I walked back where we were set up, and shouldered my bass. I tuned up, and by the time I was done, Alex and PJ had made their way back. Alex gave a 1, 2, 1, 2, 3, 4 and we jumped right into the Presstones Theme.

We played two nice long sets. Everyone in the bar was digging it, even the usuals who hated every band that played there. After we finished the second set, Roger came and paid us an extra hundred. Butch and Mugsy had collected 200. Alex and I each took 50 for our troubles, and gave PJ the rest. Roger brought over three pint glasses filled with Jack and Ice. Our instruments were still set up, but we didn't vocally say we were going to play anymore. Obviously Roger and the crowd enjoyed what they got.

If I Had Wings These Windmills Would Be Dead

We sat there drinking, chatting with a group of nannies that I recognized from both the coffee shop, and the night before. During the second set Alex had dedicated My Girl to the redhead who had been dancing up a storm. They were now chatting together in the corner. The crowd had thinned out considerable, but at about 1:30 our old roommate Pete walked in. Then came a few more nannies, and after them another old friend of mine. This period of time was known as O'Hurly's Second Wind, when all the other local bars started filtering out and the remaining partyers all congregated back at O'Hurly's.

Mugsy was telling Pete that he missed out on a great show, so Pete started egging us on.

"Come on man, you guys should play another set. If you play another set I'll help you pack up afterwards." That was all the incentive we really needed. We jumped back up to play. Mugsy went over to Roger to have him turn off the juke box, and Roger looked over at us and gave us a big thumbs up.

We started off playing Pipeline, but when we finished the regular song PJ yelled over to keep the rhythm going. Right before we got to the turnaround PJ yelled "Skip the 30's" and Alex and I hit it perfectly at the turn around. When we finished the song we instinctively jumped right back into Pipeline.

"Superstition" I yelled right before we hit the turn around, and we jumped right into our best version of it ever. When it was over we went back into Pipeline. PJ yelled out "Rumble" and Alex and I perfectly hit the first note slowing the rhythm way down. PJ started ripping the Link Wray tune like he had never ripped a tune before. At one point I swear that he jumped on a table while crashing monster chords over ferocious leads.

This went on for an hour. We kept weaving in and out of songs, always using Pipeline as the segue. We finally finished with, what else but, the Presstones Theme. It was the best we had ever played and ever sounded, and it was completely unplanned. It was the spontaneity that I had been looking for mixed perfectly with the quick in, quick out vibe PJ had always wanted.

Chuck Howe

By the end of the night my fingers were bleeding, Alex's knuckles were split open from hitting rims, and PJ looked half dead. I ended up driving PJ and his brother, who had come up by train to tape the show, back to his place in Brooklyn. The drive home, alone in the car blasting a tape of the show, as the sun rose was perfect for me. I was wide awake, and felt great. Which was a good thing, because I had to drive over 90 mph to make it back in time for work

Married

It was two o'clock in the morning and Mugsy and I were hammered. We were playing in the hard core metal band and had practiced earlier that night. Rehearsals usually started with cheap beer and ended with cheap whiskey.

O'Hurly's ended up being one of those once in a lifetime nights. We played until three in the morning, had people dancing on the bar. The whole night the drummer was absolutely mesmerized by the beautiful redhead who was obviously digging the hell out of us. I had seen her in the coffee shop before, but didn't know her well. After the gig they started talking.

Turned out Zipp was a nanny from Utah, a Mormon and really into Alex. She seemed a little insane, but then again all women did to me at that point. I didn't think much of it until a few days later.

Mugsy and I were smoking a joint. I was playing a guitar; he was banging on bongos and singing loudly. That was just what we did at two in the morning. Our only neighbors, Pearl and Bernie downstairs, were ancient. The either didn't hear us, or were afraid of the two insane kids living upstairs from them and never complained. Suddenly there was a knock. Door, Mugsy's giant german shepherd, began barking and going nuts the way he did. We weren't expecting anyone. Mugsy answered in his angry as fuck and looking to kick someone's ass mode.

It was Alex and Zipp.

"Does Chuck live here?" I heard Alex ask nervously. Neither of them knew Mugsy and the giant dog he was holding back.

"Hey Alex, what's up?" Mugsy broke out of ass kicker mode and jumped into hosting mode. He locked Door in his bedroom so he wouldn't maul anyone the way he liked to do. They looked extremely relieved to see me sitting on the couch when they came in the living room.

"Hey Chuck, sorry to show up so late. I stopped by your parent's place and they told me where you lived." I had only been there a month or two. My parents basically lived the next town over. I was sure they loved getting woken up at 1 or 2 in the morning. "Um, can you really marry people?"

"Why?"
"Because we are in love and want to get married."
"Why?"
"Well I go back to the Navy next week so I thought..."
I took a long pull from the whiskey bottle. "Are you drunk?" I asked.
"No," they both answered in unison.
Well, you got me beat. Lets's do this shit."

Bar Stools and Dreamers

Mugsy and I had taken our girlfriends out for the night. We had a great dinner, and ended up at O'Hurly's for drinks like we did almost every night. The bar was packed and it was a holiday weekend, so there were a lot of people there that we didn't know. From the moment we walked in a giant mullet head was eye balling Mugsy.

That wasn't completely uncommon. Mugsy was a big scary looking dude. Other big scary looking dudes always eye each other. I wasn't a big scary guy, so I quickly forgot about mullet head and we found a table in the back. Between two German girls, Mugsy and I, we went through a lot of beer. A lot.

Once the waitresses went off duty, we had to go up to the bar to fill our pitcher. I took the first trip and there was mullet head, eye balling everyone who walked by. I could tell he was just looking to fuck with someone. I'm not a violent guy, but I have to admit, I was kind of hoping someone would come in and kick this guy's ass. I got my beer and hurried back to the table.

By the next time the pitcher was empty, I had forgotten about mullet head and Mugsy volunteered to get the next round. Back in high school, Mugsy was known as a weight lifting bad ass. After high school he started smoking pot. Although he had mellowed out a lot, he was still pretty much a bad ass.

He was only gone for a minute when there was suddenly a huge ruckus coming from the bar. We couldn't really see what was going on, but suddenly we saw beer flying through the air and the sounds of shouts and punches. I turned to Mugsy girlfriend and said, "I think your boyfriend is in a fight."

"No'" she said in a perfectly calm voice, "I know my boyfriend is in a fight." By the time we got up front, Mugsy was on the ground with three guys hitting him with bar stools. The two girls and I rushed up and sort of just stood in between Mugsy and the guys beating him. Two of the guys dropped their stools and kind of stopped once we showed up.

Chuck Howe

The third guy was, of course, Mullet Head. He was soaking wet, covered in beer. There was a very large, bleeding cut under his eye and it was already starting to swell up. He still held a stool, wanting to hit something. You could almost see the thought processes in his eyes.

First he looked at my girlfriend, a small thin girl who wasn't much of a physical threat to anyone except for the time she accidentally hit me in the nuts with a tennis racket. He cocked back, but thought better of it. Then he looked at Mugsy's girl. I have to admit, she was a pretty tough looking girl (beautiful, but I wouldn't want to fight her) but again he thought better of it. Then he saw me. The only guy.

He smiled a little and looked like he was starting to swing the stool right down on me. I held my hands out to the side, gave a big smile and said, "Go ahead, that'll prove you're a tough guy." He actually stumbled back, as if I had hit him, and I saw the stool drop to his side. I immediately turned to Mugsy, helped him up and got him out of the door and to the car. I looked at Mugsy, his shirt was torn, but he didn't even have the slightest bruise or red mark on him. "Dude, what happened?"

"The guy looked at me funny, so I went to punch him. I forgot I had a pitcher of beer in my hand though."

WALKERS

Every town has at least one. The walking guy. They can be found anywhere, at any time. Walking. Not really going anywhere in particular, just walking. It is never a normal walk either. It's always a harsh staggering gait, or at least a hop every other step. Each quirk has something to give the walker his own style.

Mount Kisco had enough walkers to populate entire states out west. They were all shapes and sizes. Some more eccentric than others, but they all had their quirks.

The first walker I remember meeting was the "You know me" walker. He is probably still around, but he's one of the most boring of the walkers. All he did was walk around saying "You know me." There was another walker that I nicknamed Verbal after the character in "the Usual Suspects." If you saw him walking down an empty street, he had a slight limp but nothing too serious. If he was on a busy street he was all over the place. He would walk into people, with arms and legs spasming and jerking out in all directions. Not to say that he was faking, but I think he did ham it up a bit when there was an audience.

There was another walker that I could not claim for my town alone. Stretch, as Bob named him, could be seen in almost every town in Westchester. I could swear that I even saw him out in Oregon once. Stretch was an old, tall, thin gray haired black man, always sporting a purple CBS Sports jacket no matter what the weather. He walked pretty fast, tapping his umbrella along with him as he went, but he was as much a sitting man as he was a walking man. I could swear he would be sitting on a bench on one side of town, I would drive to the other side, and there he was sitting on a stone wall. The man could cruise. He walked fast but like he was not going anywhere in particular, and he probably wasn't.

The exact opposite was Little Train. He walked fast and hard and like he was on a mission from God herself. With each step he bobbed up and down so hard you would almost expect him to lift off the ground as he went up. In the corner of his mouth he always had his pipe. Both hands were shoved in the pockets of his brown blazer with his thumbs sticking out. He wore the same brown suit every day, with the vest buttoned and his bow tie perfect. He moved like a man on a mission, but all he did was circle the town. He probably got about twenty laps a day in.

Then there was the Counter. He was one of the few that I never had a conversation with, but not for a lack of trying. Counter wasn't out to meet people, he was out to count and he might even react semi-violently to anyone who tried to stop him from counting. He showed up every day and started by walking down one block, counting each step. Then he turned around and walked back down the block. He walked up and down each block four times counting the number of steps. You could hear him muttering the number as he walked past. Then he moved on to the next block. I would have loved to talk to him one day. Did the town grow in the summer and shrink in the winter? What was the biggest one-day loss or gain? Was the town bigger in the morning or afternoon?

Finally there was Mean Guy Joe. He looked like he should be standing on the bow of a ship in a storm cursing the waves. Maybe it was the wool-knit cap that always covered his head, no matter the weather. Maybe it was the look on his face. When he looked at you, you felt like he was letting you live, but could change his mind at any moment. He was out of place in a quiet landlocked suburb.

Mean Guy Joe was a regular at my coffee shop. He had a small coffee, and I learned after his first trip in that I should never leave room for milk. I should have known, a mean guy like Mean Guy Joe didn't use milk.

Like all good coffee shops we had our coffee club cards. Ten coffees got you a free one. Every time in, Mean Guy Joe would grab a coffee card and ask me to stamp it for him, he had forgotten his card at home. Every now and then he would come in with 10 cards, each with one stamp. I gave him a free coffee. We were spending a lot of money to print them, so I would save the cards that weren't badly wrinkled and reuse them.

I only learned his name was actually Joe when I offered to keep his card there and stamp it whenever he came in. I wanted to put his name on it

If I Had Wings These Windmills Would Be Dead

so others would know whose card it was, he simply replied "Joe." So as not to be confused with any other Joes, I wrote "Mean Guy Joe." After a few chats about music and books and the like, I learned that Mean Guy Joe wasn't mean at all. After that I felt bad writing "Mean Guy Joe" on his card, but that's how all of the employees knew him, and by then we had twenty or thirty customer's cards in a rolodex, and there was a Joe R and a Joe L. It was the easiest way to keep track of his free coffee.

It turned out that Joe had been a sailor. He was in the Navy during the Korean War and suffered a head injury at one point that gave him very little use of his facial muscles. That was why he always looked like he was ready to kick an ass.

We only had short conversations, but they were almost daily. I learned that he lived in a half way house for people with brain injuries. I knew a few of the other residents. One guy would always try to steal tea bags. And there was Cliff, an engineer who had been hit by a drunk driver, leaving him with both physical and mental damage. Poor Cliff seemed angry at the world and everyone in it, and I didn't really blame him. Joe had been living in half way houses for most of his life.

He really liked Jazz. If Miles Davis or Thelonious Monk was playing, you could see the faintest hint of a smile on his face, it was more in his eyes than on his lips. Every morning I would make sure there was a jazz CD in the 6 disk changer. I would put it on random play which made the odds much better that a Jazz song would come on while he was there. Occasionally he would ask me about some of the other music, too. He seemed to like Steely Dan.

One day he came in and he didn't look mean, he looked sad. He told me that he was moving to a different halfway house, one closer to a family member. His coffee card was still a long way from a free coffee, but if that was going to be his last coffee there, it was going to be free. After finishing his coffee he came over to me and held out his hand. I shook it and said goodbye.

"Thank you for talking to me. I really liked it here." He quickly turned and left. I was sad to see him go, but the feeling I got when he told me that was validation that I was on the right track for becoming the man I hoped to be.

Sao Paulo Shuffle

The trip began and ended in Sao Paulo, a sprawling metropolis where modern skyscrapers are flanked by hovels made from old bookshelves and rusted street signs. My traveling companion was Ana, my girlfriend at the time. She was Portuguese, but grew up in France. She had five sisters, four with the name Ana or Anne somewhere in their name. There was Anne Marie, Ana Maria, and Ana Dominique. My Ana was either Anne Elena or Ana Elene, depending upon when you asked her.

Her oldest sister, Anne Marie or simply Anne, lived with her French husband Roberto in Sao Paulo. He worked for a company that set him up with a huge 4-bedroom house. The entire property was walled and there was a pool with a beautiful barbeque pit and a bar. There was an armed guard on the street that would run up and open the gate allowing us to pull the car onto the property.

They had a weird dog named Pegas, short for Pegasus I assumed but never really knew. According to Ana, she was named after the horse with the horn, but that was Ana. Of course the way Roberto, Anne and Ana called the dog sounded to me like they were saying "Big Ass." So whenever I would call the dog I would say "Com'ere Big Ass. Thassa Good Big Ass. Gooood Big Ass." The dog loved the attention. Roberto and Anne must have thought I really loved dogs, but Ana had been with me long enough to actually know what I was saying.

About three days after we got there I was really in need of some good old marijuana. Since I was in a completely new environment, with people who never smoked, it would be a few days before I really needed any but I could feel the urge building already. We had hiked around Ibirapuerra Park on the second day, and a bunch of guys were sitting around smoking, but I resisted.

Roberto and Anne were at work, so Ana and I were hanging out by the pool. Big Ass started barking from inside so I told Ana that I would take her for a walk and pick up some cigarettes on my trip. Innocent enough. I had no other plans in mind. She thanked me for going; it meant she didn't have to. Her sister lived in a neighborhood of small estates. There was a small but beautiful park, and then a main road with many stores and a drag race at 2 every morning.

As Big Ass and I left I noticed the guard wasn't in his normal little booth. I thought nothing of it, he was often asked to help with things in the neighborhood. As I turned the corner to the park, I noticed a group of 6 or 7 younger looking guys huddled around near a group of bushes. Suddenly I was thinking of danger. I certainly didn't look like I had money in the way I dressed. I looked like most of the Brazilians I had met so far, so I wasn't worried about looking like a tourist. But it was kind of intimidating to see in a foreign country known for kidnappings and worse.

I was somewhat relieved when I saw the guard from our neighborhood sitting with them. The guard sort of waved at me and I waved back as I passed. It wasn't until I passed that I smelled that familiar smell of marijuana. Big Ass and I went to the store, got our smokes, and I was basically dragging Big Ass back to the park as fast as I could hoping they'd still be there. They were, but the guard wasn't with them. Suddenly high school Spanish splashed into my head. I hoped bad Spanish sounded something like Portuguese.

"Amigos, Ayuda me pra favor (I knew the pra instead of por part) Yo no fume pra tres dias." They all looked at me funny. One of them started laughing.

"Do you mean that you need help because you haven't smoked in three days?" One of them spoke in near perfect English.

"Um yeah." I had a cigarette in my hand, so I figured he knew what I meant.

"Well sit right down."

Half hour later I stumbled back into the house. Ana came running in from the kitchen looking worried, until she took one look at my face. "How the hell did you get high?" She wasn't against me smoking, she smoked from time to time herself. It was more shock than anything. She probably figured I was lost or kidnapped. Instead I walked in blazed out of my mind with a twenty bag in my pocket.

Einfahrt Freihaiten

I stood on the platform, naked, as the train I wanted to take to Amsterdam pulled into the station. Two policeman/soldiers stood on either side of me holding on to automatic weapons sifting through my bag and my paper work. I wondered what the inside of a German jail looked like. I was afraid I was going to find out.

It all started a few years earlier, at the coffee shop. Nannies from all over the world would come in and I soon found out that if you give a girl from Germany enough free coffee, she became your girlfriend. She was only here for a year and though she wasn't the sweetest or kindest girl, she was a lot of fun and really cute. So sure, no problem. We had a great time whenever we went out.

It was supposed to be over when she went back to Germany, and it was, but we stayed in touch. We both started dating other people. We both broke up with other people. She came back to visit for a week and stayed with me and we had a great time again. After she got back to Germany she called and told me to come out there for a visit. I had time off, so I got myself a plane ticket.

From the second I got there she had an expression on her face like "What are you doing here Asshole?"

Immediately I realized that when she was in New York, she was on vacation and German people on vacation were a lot of fun. German people at home were not. They had very strict laws and rules and they actually followed them. In America, when they were here visiting, they could break whatever rule they wanted and it was fun. I took her to bars when she was 19 years old. But when I went over there I was getting yelled at for jaywalking. One day my innate ability to find weed led me to some guy she didn't know. I smoked a bowl and she acted like I was the most evil person on the face of the earth, so of course I bought a big bag from him.

Finally one night we got into a big fight and I just left her place and went to the first bar I saw. I finished the only bottle of Jack Daniels that they had, so I went to the next bar. It was a small German town, but even the smallest town in Germany has lots of bars. I finished all of their Jack at the second bar, drank some of their Beam, and then went to another bar. The girl, her sister and a friend show up at the third bar.

"How'd you know I was here," I asked.

"I called the bar and asked if there was a crazy American there and they said yes. We were supposed to go out to dinner together tonight."

"So order some food. I am drinking."

Our waiter was obviously gay, and she made some comment about it. Throughout my stay in Germany I was noticing a lot of statements that I never noticed her making in America. At one point we had driven past an apartment building and she pointed out that was where all the people from Turkey lived. "There was never any crime here before the Turks came."

Yeah, sure. There had never been any crime committed against anyone in Germany before the Turks came. Well, maybe it was legal to kill millions of Jews in Germany in the 40's. And I guessed the medieval skeleton in the cage hanging from the steeple of the church in Muenster was only there by choice.

She said something about how she hoped I had gotten rid of my weed. When I said no she said something about not wanting it in her house.

"Yeah, don't worry; I am not stepping foot in your house again."

"Well then where are you going to stay?" she asked as the waiter came with their food.

I just kind of lost it. Between the whiskey and the weed I had enough. "I can stay with you, right?" I asked the waiter. He looked at me a bit confused so I jumped up on the table and started singing Blue Sunday by the Doors at the top of my lungs to him.

She got super pissed and pulled me off the table. It was the same song I had stood on a bar and sang to her back in America. She just grabbed me and yelled, "NO, you're coming home with me. All your things are there."

"I don't fucking care, I'm not going back to your house," I replied, but I

If I Had Wings These Windmills Would Be Dead

was a little too drunk and she finally got me to agree to go back.

I passed out on her couch and when I woke up in the morning she was already up. She gave me the evil eye and said "Now I am going to have a talk with you." She started talking about it being her town and her friends and how I had embarrassed her.

"Well I'm on vacation and don't know anyone here, so fuck you. I'm out of here." She didn't believe I would leave. I was supposed to be in Germany for another week, but I grabbed my suitcase and art bag and left. There was a Goodwill box right across from her place, so I just dropped the suitcase there so I didn't have to lug it around. It was raining pretty hard and I had to cross a farm and a bunch of streets to get to the bus stop, but I finally found it. Right as I sat down to wait for the bus, she pulled up in her car.

"Where do you think you're going?"

"Bus to the Muenster train station, and then I don't know, Amsterdam I guess."

"I have your book, you left your book." It was Still Life with Woodpecker by Tom Robbins.

"Read it, you might learn something."

She threw it out of the window at me. It landed a few feet away in a puddle.

"PICK IT UP!" She yelled at me just as the bus pulled up. She was stopped in the bus lane and the bus beeped.

"Fuck you, my bus is here," I yelled at her and she drove away.

I got on the bus thinking "That's awesome. She littered. I just made her break the law." I took the bus into Muenster, walked in the train station and I knew I was a wreck. My hair all over the place, my clothes soaking wet. I saw on the board there was a train leaving soon for Amsterdam. I bought a ticket from an agent who looked more than a little scared of me. I got to the platform and found a payphone. The cash machine kept giving me money, but wouldn't give me a balance and I had no idea how much money I had left. I tried to call my bank to get a balance but none of the phone numbers on my card were working. I kept getting a German recording I didn't understand. By the third time I slammed the phone down and yelled "Fuck!"

"PASSPORT PLEASE!" I heard in a thick German accent from behind me. I looked down and saw the two automatic weapons. I slowly turned and saw two German cops looking really pissed at me.

"PASSPORT, PLEASE!" he said again.

"How do you know I'm not from Germany?"

"Passport and plane ticket home. Let me see them now!"

I opened my art bag and pulled out my passport and ticket. I had some pot left and a little glass pipe, but it was tucked in a part of my bag that was hard to find. When the other cop grabbed the bag and started pulling stuff out, however, I thought for sure that he would find it.

The first cop finished looking at my paper work, looked at me and said, "Strip."

"Right here?" I asked and he nodded. I stripped down to my boxers.

"Off," he said using the gun to point to my boxers. Of course I dropped them right down just as my train pulled into the station. As I stood there naked he asked "What the fuck is wrong with you?"

"Dude, I learned not to piss off a German girl."

Immediately they both started laughing. "Pull your pants back up and catch your train, you poor bastard."

As they started walking away, I realized I still hadn't reached my bank. I figured I would ask the cops if I had to dial something special to get through. "Hey! Excuse me but..." I yelled as I kind of started running towards where they were going.

They turned around with the guns again aimed at me shouting "YOU DO NOT RAISE YOUR VOICE TO A GERMAN OFFICER!!"

If I Had Wings These Windmills Would Be Dead

"OK. Never mind," I said as I finished buttoning my shirt. I got on the train, and had never been happier to leave a city in my life. I would arrive in Amsterdam in a few hours. I later found out that I had a lot more money in the bank than I thought which was good, because I only had the clothes that were now back on my back.

At Least I'm Enjoying the Ride

I had only been to her grave twice. The last time was on the day of her funeral. The first time was about a month before she died. She looked weak, and grimaced in pain when she moved, but like always, Michelle was in a great mood. She knew that she didn't have very long left. She actually didn't want me coming out and seeing her like that, but I know she was glad to see me once I got there. The calls had been getting less frequent, and I hadn't seen her in a couple of years, but when she called and said she didn't think she had much longer I came running.

It was a strange visit to the cemetery. I was in shock, looking at the grave of a friend. I stared at the ground knowing she would soon be underneath the grass. Michelle was looking at the mountains and the trees and the beautiful peaceful view around the cemetery. I couldn't see any of that; I could only see a small patch of land that would one day swallow her. I was feeling very guilty about not visiting more often. I kept trying to speak, but no words came out. Finally she broke the silence.

"Isn't it beautiful?" She asked, using too much energy as she swirled her thin frame around, barely managing to get her skirt to twirl. She steadied herself on her cane as she came to a stop. I put my arm around her to help support her. There was almost nothing there. When I met her she had the physique of a true outdoor sports lover. She was thin, but it was a very muscular thin. Now she was an emaciated thin.

"Yes, a great view." All I could think of was that she wouldn't be able to see it from under the dirt and grass. "Just save your energy, OK?"

"Save it for what? I have been saving it, saving it so I could dance." She did a little spin towards me and grabbed my free hand. "Dance with me?"

"I am not going to dance on your grave," I replied with a laugh.

"Oh, you are just taking all the fun out of dying," she said with a smile. "Besides, it isn't my grave yet, just a good place to dance." She began gently swaying in my arms and I couldn't resist. I could never argue with her logic, so soon enough, I was dancing on a beautiful piece of grass with Michelle and enjoying an amazing view.

41

I had known Diamond Jim the Drummer since middle school. We played together off and on through the years. He knew of a studio in town, and knew that I had been a bit down and out, so he set up a weekly jam session. Guy, who I knew and heard play, but had never played with, was on guitar most weeks. It was a fun little jam. We got to play rock tunes, drink beer and smoke weed without being bothered by anyone.

One week Diamond Jim told us that he invited a guy he worked with to come play. He worked selling life insurance, so we really weren't sure who would show up. He told us that Al was cool. He was a bit older than we were, but he smoked. "He'll fit right in," Jim assured us.

Jim was right. He was a small thin Italian guy whose deep bass voice boomed out over the entire room. He had a big laugh and a friendly smile. He was a good guitarist, not great. He worked really well with Guy though and led us through a nice little funk jam that gave me lots of room to explore on bass. I liked him right away.

He had to get home early the first night, so I didn't get to talk to him too much, but he was the first one there the next week. I got there early too, and we had a chance to chat while everyone else was still setting up. While chatting he mentioned that he used to be in the music business. Dance music to be more precise. He mentioned being a part of the first rave scene back in the late 80's. I had been to a few raves in the 90's. Fun, but I had more fun at Phish shows.

Just before we went to start the jam, he told me he still did some dance stuff from home. He had enjoyed my bass playing, and wanted to know if I wanted to come over and work on a few tracks with him. I said sure, it wasn't my usual music, but I had found I always learned a lot when I went out of my comfort zone. I gave him my number and we went in and had a great jam.

A few nights later I went to his house. He had a nice little basement office set up, complete with Gold records on the wall and a signed photo of Robert Plant. He saw me looking at it.

"Yeah, I worked for Swan Song records back when I was in high school, and then moved on to Atlantic after that."

We sat at his desk and he played me a song he was working on. I could see the different instruments on different tracks on the computer screen as the music played. There was a heavy dance beat, with layers of various keyboard sounds over it. I had never seen music displayed like that before. It blew my mind.

"Before we record your bass, we should bone up," he said. I wasn't sure what Al meant by that. I knew he was married; I had just met his wife. When he pulled out a bag of weed and a rolling paper, I felt much better. Bone up meant smoke weed, it made perfect sense. For a minute I wasn't too sure.

The bass parts he wanted me to add were simple. I did three songs the first night. He could have easily played the bass himself, or added a synth bass, but he wanted me to do it. He burned me the CD right there on the spot. I was able to listen on my way home, it was amazing. I told Al I had been working on a few acoustic tunes of my own, and he offered to help me record them the next week.

I had been becoming more withdrawn over the years, but Al's place was a place I immediately felt safe. I would end up going back at least once a week for the next few years. I would help with bass and sometimes even keyboards for some of his stuff, and he would help me with mine. My own stuff was strange, but it amused him. When he went away over the summer, I would take care of his dog and spend hours in his office recording away.

Eventually I got my own home studio set up on my computer, and Al got a job doing sound for the United Nations, so we didn't get to see each other as much as we had. We would still get together for jams with Diamond Jim, but Jim had gotten married and the jams became less frequent.

He was always working and thinking music though. A friend of mine was doing booking at a club in Connecticut and one day I was lucky enough to be backstage at a Black Crowes show. Al called while I was hanging with some of the guys in the opening band. I hadn't talked to him in a while so I went out into the hall so we could chat.

If I Had Wings These Windmills Would Be Dead

He told me he was in the emergency room. His back had been killing him all day and his wife, who worked for a cardiologist, was afraid it was his heart. He was waiting to go in for an x-ray, but he didn't seem too worried. I told him where I was and he was immediately thinking of acts he knew that he could try booking there. Finally the Doctor came in so we got off the phone. I went back to the backstage party and foolishly didn't think much of it. Al didn't seem too worried. I was sure he was going to be fine.

About two days later I got an e-mail from him, I could see it was sent out to a bunch of people. In it he talked about what a great life he had, and how he was so happy to have his wife by his side. I immediately dialed Al's number.

The phone went right to voicemail. His phone never went right to voicemail. I called again and again and it was always the same, right to voicemail. Finally I called Diamond Jim.

I could hear his tears before he even spoke. Al had lung cancer. It was aggressive and it was advanced. He did not have much time. I couldn't believe this was happening. Al had so much life, so much energy. He was such a caring soul, anytime you had any news, good or bad, his first thought was about helping.

The doctor was right about the diagnosis. Before the month was even over, Al had passed away.

I went to his wake. He had already been cremated. It tore me apart, but I had to say goodbye. He had left me a message the night before he passed. He sounded great; he was excited to see me later in the week. I couldn't believe it when I heard he was gone the very next day. I had to go. I had to see his wife, tell her how much I loved them both. How much they both meant to me. I wanted to say all of that and more, but "I love you and I'm so sorry" or some other all too often repeated phrase came out.

Bob came with me. He had been to Al's a few times and had met the whole family. Al and I even got him to play some guitar on a few tracks, but Bob was even worse than I was with death, so when I suggested leaving after only being there for ten minutes, he jumped up from his seat. I had hoped to see Diamond Jim, but I had to leave. Halfway home Jim called saying he was just getting there. I felt really guilty, but I couldn't go back.

Al was one of the biggest influences in my opening up and recording my own music. He always pushed me to write stories, he always encouraged me in every way possible, but I just couldn't do it anymore. I virtually gave up playing music and writing. My number one fan was gone; I didn't see a purpose to it anymore.

The Vibes

For a very long time after the Dead show in Oregon, I had stayed far away from psychedelics of all sorts. I thought that they were evil and the cause of the depression that I was entering and then fully encased in. But eventually I started experimenting again. It really was just experimenting because it was always very small controlled doses, in very safe controlled environments. I didn't take LSD again until about two weeks after Al died. I took it almost to make myself freak out. But I only took a very small amount, and ended up having a wonderful time. There were no great truths. There were no trippy hallucinations. There was a good time and a slightly warped sense of reality.

And then came the Gathering of the Vibes. It was a beautiful friendly place. I knew right away I was at home. I had stayed away from festivals for a long time. They made me too happy, and I didn't want to be happy. There were twenty good bands I really wanted to see, all at one place. We got hooked up with cheap tickets and VIP passes. What could be better?

It took a while for Sabrina and me to figure out where we were supposed to go after we arrived at Seaside Park. Other friends would meet us later and wherever we ended up would become base camp. We completely lucked out and were put right up against the "in and out parking" for the campground. Sabrina could keep her car there, and the second car could come and go as those in our group needed to go the forty five minutes back home. I did it more than I thought I would and I'm glad. The festival was four days long. I could get home, sleep a few hours, shower and be back for the second band of the day.

There were three guys camped next to us. We had friendly introductions, smoked a bowl, had a real good conversation, saw some music together, and smoked another bowl, and they became our best friends ever. Luck, like the sun, was shining on us from moment one.

The first night I drank some beers, smoked some weed and enjoyed the show. Shit was going on all around me. Anything I wanted was there. I knew that. I didn't want it yet, but it was good to know it was there.

Chuck Howe

The scene was perfect. The hike back to the camp was perfect. This was my place. Here I could be one of the 30,000 other Kings and Queens of the Vibes.

The second night I was ready to explore. I had already seen Sharon Jones, Steve Kimock, Caravan of Thieves and Robert Randolf. I was ready for more. I was ready for Further. I found someone who had the good clean "Family" acid, just like back in Oregon. It hadn't kicked in yet when Bobby and Phil hit the stage. I hadn't seen them since that 1993 Grateful Dead show. With the start of the first song we rushed up closer than I had ever dreamed at any of the Grateful Dead shows I had ever been to. There was Phil Lesh, right in front of me. I was in Heaven.

Then a glow stick came out of nowhere and hit me between my eye and the eye socket. It grotesquely stuck there for a split second until the glow stick popped out before I had a chance to grab it. It didn't hurt too badly, but my eye started to tear. I had Reed take a look to make sure there was no blood or obvious damage to the eye. There wasn't, it just stung a bit.

I kept rubbing my eye, but the next song began, I cheered and threw my arms in the air, then back to rubbing the eye. It didn't really hurt and I knew if I kept rubbing it I might actually do damage, especially since the acid was starting to kick in. It was good clean acid, I could already tell.

Suddenly there was a hand on my shoulder. I turned and there was a short, bald, tie-dye wearing New York/New Jersey looking guy. If you saw him in Manhattan you'd expect to hear him say stuff like "Fuck you buddy," or "Your momma's a whore." Never in Manhattan had a guy like this apologized to anyone. At least that's how he looked, I could be wrong but he didn't look like the apologizing type. I really had no idea of what he wanted from me except maybe a hit off the pipe that had passed me just a few moments ago.

"Hey buddy, I'm really sorry. I hit you in the eye with a glow stick. It slipped out as I went to throw it up in the air and went straight into your eye. I feel horrible." He didn't need to say anything. It was a concert. Glow sticks get thrown; I knew the risks coming in. Besides,

If I Had Wings These Windmills Would Be Dead

it didn't even really hurt anymore, I just kept touching it to make sure my eye was still there.

"That's OK, man. You're super cool for apologizing; you didn't have to do that. My eye is fine." I gave him a one arm hug and he took it. Again that would never happen between us in the "real world".

"No it's not OK, I'm sorry. Here, take a vicoden. It'll help even if it doesn't hurt." I took it and thanked him. I looked at the plain pill in my hand. I never really popped pills, but I had friends that did. I'm sure this would make someone's night.

Reed had witnessed, but not heard our exchange. I turned to him and tried to hand him the pill. "That was the nicest guy who ever hit me in the eye," I told him, "Do you want this vicoden?" He looked at it, looked at me and told me I should take it, after all, I earned it.

I swallowed it and I had fun. I spent the rest of the night dancing and walking at the same time. I hit every corner of the festival grounds that I could find. I smiled at everyone. I danced with a bunch of them. I know I kissed at least two women along the way. I don't know if the vicoden had any effect on me through the acid, but the love did.

When the night ended we trekked back to camp, where a psychedelic Dixieland band was playing. They rocked. I danced and smiled some more. The trip had been great, the trip had been fun, but it hadn't been fulfilling. I had already made up my mind. The next night I was going to trip, and I was going to trip hard. Screw that deep dark feeling that I would one day freak out in a large crowd and end up hospitalized. If that was what was going to happen, then so be it. I needed to trip face.

On Saturday July 31st 2010, I woke up still feeling the effects of the acid a little bit. I got a call that a buddy was pulling in and didn't know where we were. He hadn't pulled into the camping lot yet so I met him at the entrance as he was going through security. He had to wait for someone on a golf cart to guide him in; they didn't want any campers getting run over. My buddy had brought my banjo, so I grabbed that and jumped on the back of the golf cart so I could let him know where to go. Confusing I know, try figuring all that out on acid.

As we made our way past the beach and then through the camp

ground I jammed out some psycho blues on the banjo. Everyone we passed gave a thumbs up. Every thumbs up made my smile grow bigger. I knew it was going to be another good day.

I went and saw the band Galactic without taking anything, except some gourmet ganja treats and smoking some hash oil. I made sure I saw a few bands "sober" each day just in case I got too screwed up later on. I wanted to remember something at least. I took the first hit of a different, more "mellow" acid than the night before. When I was first starting to feel the effects I took more of the stronger stuff. The trip was happening by the end of the Keller Williams set. Next up was Primus. I had never seen them before, but I knew they gave a special show. Suddenly I found myself with the opportunity to take Ecstasy. Not the Molly that was going around but X. It was good stuff. One friend had been on it for a while and loved it. Why not add it to the mix? I mixed acid and X once before when I was younger, and had a great time. Pop went the blue star pill.

Then Primus hit the stage. There was a VIP only dance floor right in the center of the venue and it was elevated just slightly to give a perfect view of the stage. We got up there and started dancing. Moving my head while dancing started doing weird things to my stomach and I knew I was starting to roll. The joy of the MDMA, one of the main ingredients in Ecstacy doesn't kick in first. It's the speed and the narcotics that hit you first, and it rocks your body. I had forgotten about this. The physical effects just tweaked my mind where the acid was really starting to twist things around.

Les Claypool suddenly hit an arpeggio that I just couldn't understand. His bass line seemed to shatter the air around me. It was hard to breath. The music was just too strange for me. After taking a hit off the bowl being passed I thought I might calm down but it didn't happen. I sat down on the bouncing dance floor. My mind twisted as much as my body. Fully rolling and fully tripping "It's just the drugs" was my new mantra. I suddenly questioned my existence. I felt myself leaving my mind. This was going to be it. I knew it. This was going to be the trip I didn't come back from. It was the trip that would get me locked away in a loony bin, but what did that even

If I Had Wings These Windmills Would Be Dead

mean? I wasn't in my mortal coil; I was a stranger outside myself who knew nothing about that person curled in a ball on the dance stage.

Suddenly there was a tap on my shoulder. "Do you have any rolling papers? I got weed, but no papers." I looked at him with shock at first. Did I know him? Was he real? Was he me and I him? "Do you have any papers?" he repeated. And suddenly I knew something. I knew I had no papers. I then knew everything again. Some random guy had just saved me from collapse. The first roll was coming to an end. My body felt great. My mind was suddenly crystal clear once again. It didn't even feel like I was on acid. We smoked my new friend up with a pipe since no one had papers. The dance floor was still kind of moving, I still felt weird and Primus was still playing really weird stuff. I went back to our "In show staging area" between the entrance to the VIP tent and Restroomworld. Whenever anyone needed finding, they were there.

I was very aware and happy and clear jamming to Primus playing Pink Floyd's "In the Flesh" and a few other songs when the second roll hit. I always remembered the first roll being the worst and the second roll not being so bad. This one hit me twice as hard. Again I rolled up in a ball. Again my mind warped with the acid's reaction to physical pain. This time there was no doubt. I was gone. I was now a demon. Rage filled me. I wanted to kill the world in an instant. I saw everyone who I thought had ever done me wrong and I was ready to get up and fight every one of them. I was about to scream and go wild when the music seemed to suddenly stop.

It was peaceful and quiet. Deep Banana Blackout would be playing next. I knew that and knew my friends wanted to see it. All I needed and wanted was to go back to the tent. From the tent I knew where the EMS station was. I saw Reed standing in front of me. Everyone was ready to head to Deep Banana and I think he was asking me if I was ready.

"Please. Get me water and take me back to the tent. I'll be OK. I just need to make sure I get back there." Without saying a word Reed grabbed a water bottle out of someone's hand and gave it to me. I was sweating balls and so was he, but he let me put my arm around his shoulder and we began walking. He never told any of our other friends what was up, he knew I just needed to get back, and he knew he'd find them at Deep Banana or he wouldn't. That didn't really matter and he knew it. I needed a friend and that was all that mattered to him.

We didn't say much to each other as we started walking, but I already knew what I would do once he left me at our tent. I would leave a note on the car, and go to the EMS station, and asked to be committed. I loved the world, and I was about to do something to hurt myself or other people and I knew that. I might end up like the naked tasered guy that Sabrina and I had seen earlier in the day. But why bother even going to EMS. I really didn't matter to anyone or anything. Or did I? I was feeling very guilty and very low. I was worried I had abandoned both Michelle and Al. I felt like I was a terrible person and only deserved terrible things to happen to me.

"Do I matter? Am I a friend?" It was a simple question that I was afraid to ever ask, but somehow it slipped out of my lips.

Reed stopped walking, grabbed me and hugged me like only a true friend can. He told me all the words of love I ever need to hear a friend say. Not a lover, not a family member. A friend. I knew he meant it and I knew right away that I had great friends and family that have always wanted to help me and I have never let them.

I thought about the people who I thought hurt me. I thought about the people I thought I hurt. A lot of people were in both groups. I thought about the people that I absolutely hated, and I had been filled with hate for a while. It was easy to hate people. I suddenly realized that there was a time when I loved each and every one of them.

I thought about both Al and Michelle, they both loved me. Even if I had wronged them in any way, they would have forgiven me if they were still here. They would have wished me nothing but good things. In an instant, instead of hate and sadness and confusion there was an amazing feeling of joy and happiness. We were at the tent. My friend made me assure him that I was fine. A few of our neighbors were back. I never heard him but I was sure he asked them to check up on me. I just sat there, almost unable to move. I could hear the music but

If I Had Wings These Windmills Would Be Dead

it was far away. I felt joy.

The MDMA in the Ecstasy was kicking the euphoria into high gear. That was helping to steer the psychedelic effects of the acid to a really good place. All the good people in my life and all the kind things people had done for me flashed in my mind. As I sat there deep down happy for the first time in decades the final roll started to hit. I wasn't afraid this time. I felt the internal twisting and realized my water bottle was empty. My voice and body were shot. I couldn't move a muscle and I needed water. Just then I felt a bump and a heard a voice say "sorry." My neighbor had gone to his car at the perfect moment.

"Please water," I gasped and there was a bottle in my hand almost instantly. I could barely lift my head to look at him, but I was wide awake. He bent down close to me and asked if I was OK.

"Yes. Feeling awesome just exhausted." A few minutes later I felt a plate in my hand. There were some pieces of cut up fruit on it. They were the best tasting things I have ever eaten in my life. I don't even know if I tried to breathe a thank you, but my voice was gone.

By the time everyone got back to the camp I was on my feet and smiling from ear to ear. The dixieland band was playing right near us again and they sounded great. We all hung out and ate food and bs'ed for a while. I was fully planning on sleeping there and it was already 5 in the morning when Reed said he had to drive home to pick up his girl in the morning. I really didn't want to leave. I thought with all I had already been through, if I went home I wouldn't come back.

The final day was not that super special to me; I had seen most of the bands I really wanted to. I just thought I would fall asleep and not wake up for over 24 hours. But I knew Reed needed help to stay awake on the ride home, so I went. It was scary, he likes to doze off at the drop of the hat and I was fighting to keep him awake the whole ride. If there was any way that I could have done it, I would have driven, but that was the worst idea in the world.

We got home. I feel asleep smiling. I woke up without an alarm clock four hours later and went right back to the Festival and danced.

Life became a whole lot better after I decided that it was OK to be happy.

Solo

I had played live many times before. It had been twenty years of bar gigs and parties. I had been part of a house band and recorded many songs. But I was just the bass player. Occasionally I was a percussion player. Once or twice I played some banjo or rhythm guitar in a band. It was never my lyrics, and very rarely my music. I had never walked out on stage alone, with just an acoustic guitar and my voice.

I had spent years sitting on my couch or my stone wall playing an acoustic guitar and singing away. I would play a song for a friend, or band-mate if I wanted our band to play a song. I had begun recording some of my own tunes with Al helping out, but when Al passed away, I just didn't have the drive to record the way that I did before.

I had over 100 original songs that no one had ever heard, as well as countless covers I felt I could pull out at any moment. There was no reason not to try to go out and play them for others. Friends kept telling me about an open mic night at Lucy's, a local bar. When I was growing up it was a real dive bar. I really didn't think I'd want to go back in there. Everywhere I went, people were raving about Lucy's. My friend Richie had played there before so I asked him about it.

"You get three songs, and should have an acoustic/electric guitar." I had just bought a classical acoustic/electric. It was actually lining up a little too perfectly. I just had to narrow it down to three songs. I choose six to practice all weekend leading up to the Monday night open mic. This way I had a few choices and could see what kind of crowd it was before deciding.

Monday came. I got plenty of sleep. Sign up began at 8:30. I showered and was ready by 7:00. I picked up the guitar for another run through of all of my songs. None of them felt right. I tried a few others. My fingers fumbled along the fret board. 8:30 came and went and I was still sitting on my couch. By ten I had gone through 20 songs, all on my couch. The next day I woke up kicking myself for not going. I practiced all week, but this time only three songs. My three newest songs. Monday came and I was ready by 7 again. I started practicing again. This time my voice kept cracking. I don't have the best voice anyway, so it was bothering the hell out of me. Again a Monday night came and went and I had only played to my four walls.

The next week I didn't practice. That Monday came. I didn't shower. I wasn't ready for anything. The clock started approaching 8:30 and I found myself putting my guitar in my car and actually getting in it. My car actually made it to Pleasantville and parked behind the bar. I left the guitar in the car, and made my way inside.

It was a pretty nice sized room. The bar was in the middle on one side. The stage was in front of the big front windows. A guy who looked to be about my age was setting up microphones and speakers. The place wasn't too crowded yet, but I could already tell it was a nice mix of young and old.

The bartender looked like he could be a badass if you pissed him off, but he had a warm welcoming smile and introduced himself as John the moment I stepped up to the bar. Not only did he have mutton chops, he rocked the mutton chops and made them look good. I liked him right away. He pointed me in the direction of the signup sheet. There were already 5 names on it before I got to it. That was good; I would have enough time to get a few drinks in me before it was time to play.

Petey Hop, the guy who ran the open mic night came on first and played a bunch of tunes. He had a great voice and displayed amazing guitar work. He was awesome. I almost felt like scratching my name from the list. There was no way I was ready to play after him. He finished his set and called up the first name on the list.

The guy sucked, But Petey gave him lots of encouragement and got him a pretty nice hand when he was done. It made me feel a lot better about what I was going to play. Suddenly I realized I hadn't really thought about what I was going to play. The second guy came out and he was pretty good, but I was too busy worried about what my set was going to be to pay attention. I got another drink. This time, a scotch. It didn't help. My stomach was jumping inside of me. The third person was almost as good as Petey. I started getting nervous again.

If I Had Wings These Windmills Would Be Dead

The two people right before me were both very mellow and boring. Not bad singers or musicians, they just didn't hold my interest.

That clinched it for me. I was going to play three comedic songs. I had some deep meaningful tunes, but after sitting through two boring sets, we needed something different. I decided to start with "Am I Drunk Yet" a song about getting drunk at a bar. I figured it would go over nicely with the crowd. As the guy before me finished his last song I felt the nerves build up to a peak, Petey called my name. I grabbed my guitar, walked up to the stage, looked at the crowd as he plugged in my guitar, and the nerves went away.

Thank you to those who helped in editing,
especially Bud Smith, Frani Grover, Randy Howe,
Chris DiBaccari, Aaron Dietz and Emilie Rappoport.

I would also like to thank my Parents, my Grandmother,
my Brother, my entire family and all of my friends
especially Ana, Todd, Andy, Bud and Jessica
for inspiring and encouraging me.
And a special thank you to my mother for being my
first editor through 12 years of school.

And a very special dedication to Erin McParland.
I have never met a more beautiful human being, inside and out.
Thank you for reminding me of how lucky I am every single day.

CPSIA information can be obtained
at www.ICGtesting.com
Printed in the USA
LVOW12s1035110417
530399LV00018B/783/P